SPECTRUM®

Language Arts

Grade 6

Published by Spectrum®
an imprint of Carson-Dellosa Publishing LLC
Greensboro, NC

Spectrum®
An imprint of Carson-Dellosa Publishing LLC
P.O. Box 35665
Greensboro, NC 27425 USA

ISBN 978-0-7696-5306-8

09-140137811

Table of Contents Grade 6

Chapter 1 Grammar

Parts of Speech

Sentences

Table of Contents, continued

Chapter 2 Mechanics

Capitalization

Punctuation

Lesson 1.2 Regular Plural Nouns

Try It

Use the lines to explain how the nouns were made into their plural forms. The first one is done for you.

Column A	Column B	
match	matches	*If the noun ends in ch, add an es.*
eyebrow	eyebrows	
volcano	volcanoes	
wolf	wolves	
trophy	trophies	
toothbrush	toothbrushes	
fax	faxes	
sheriff	sheriffs	
studio	studios	
kiss	kisses	

Lesson 1.3 Irregular Plural Nouns

Irregular plural nouns do not have a pattern for changing from singular to plural. These nouns and their plural spellings have to be learned.

Singular noun:
child
foot
tooth

Plural noun:
children
feet
teeth

Some irregular nouns do not change at all when they are in the plural form. These forms also have to be learned.

Singular noun:
fish
deer
moose

Plural noun:
fish
deer
moose

The best way to learn these plural forms is by reading, writing, and practicing. Sometimes, when you read or hear these words used incorrectly, you will be able to tell if they are spelled incorrectly.

Find It
Write the irregular plural noun form of the following singular nouns on the lines provided. Use a dictionary if you need help.

1. ox _____

2. trout _____

3. man _____

4. series _____

5. axis _____

6. mouse _____

7. sheep_____

8. salmon_____

9. woman _____

10. crisis _____

11. oasis _____

12. radius_____

Lesson 1.3 Irregular Plural Nouns

Proof It
Correct the mistakes in the use of plural nouns using proofreading marks.

> *e* – delete words or letters
> ∧ – insert words or letters

Have you ever thought about what happens to injured mice, gooses, deer, mooses, or other wildlife when they are sick or injured? If they are lucky, they might be found by someone who knows about wildlife rehabilitation centers. Wildlife rehabilitation centers are places that care for sick or injured wild animals. They care for the animals until they can be released back into the wild. Sometimes, they take care of farm animals, too. This might include oxes or sheepes. Even species of fishes, like trout, salmons, and codes can be cared for and nursed back to health. Wildlife rehabilitation centers are wonderful places greatly needed by communities, especially as our cities extend farther into the wild. You can visit these centers and learn more about them. You might even want to volunteer!

Try It
Write a fictional paragraph using as many of the irregular plural nouns on pages 10 and 11 as you can.

_____

_____

_____

_____

_____

_____

_____

_____

_____

_____

Lesson 1.4 Personal Pronouns

A **pronoun** is a word used in place of a noun.

A **subject pronoun** can be the subject of a sentence.
I, you, he, she, and *it* are subject pronouns.

      I found the ball.   *You* found the ball.
      He found the ball.   *She* found the ball.
      It is my favorite sport.

An **object pronoun** can be the object of a sentence.
Me, you, him, her, and *it* are object pronouns.

      Matt gave the ball to *me*.   Matt gave the ball to *you*.
      Matt gave the ball to *him*.   Matt gave the ball to *her*.
      Matt threw *it*.

Possessive pronouns show possession.
My, mine, your, yours, his, her, hers, and *its* are possessive pronouns.

      Anna gave *my* ball to Matt.
      Anna gave *mine* to Matt. (includes the word ball)

The plural forms of personal pronouns include:

      Subject: *we, you, they*   *We/You/They* found the ball.
      Object: *us, you, them*   Matt gave the ball to *us/you/them*.
      Possessive: *our, ours, your, yours, their, theirs*
      Matt gave *our ball/ours/your ball/yours/their ball/theirs* to Anna.

Complete It
Complete the following sentences by choosing the best word in parentheses. Then, write what type of pronoun (subject, object, or possessive) it is on the line after the sentences.

1. _____ (I, Me) like movies. _____

2. Gloria handed the flowers to _____ (his, her) sister. _____

3. Stephanie wanted _____ (him, he) to ask her to the dance. _____

4. The teacher gave John _____ (his, her) paper back. _____

5. _____ (It, You) is the team's favorite food. _____

6. _____ (Him, You) are the quarterback on the football team. _____

7. The teacher wanted _____ (me, he) to try out for the play. _____

8. _____ (Her, She) likes volleyball better than softball. _____

Lesson 1.4 Personal Pronouns

Identify It

The following skit contains subject, object, and possessive plural pronouns. Identify what each boldfaced plural pronoun is replacing on the line. Then, write whether the pronoun is a subject, object, or possessive on the line. The first one has been done for you.

Matt and Anna are on **their** _____Matt and Anna, possessive_____ way to the

park to play. On the way, **they** _____ meet Andrew and Stephanie.

"**We** _____ are on **our**

_____ way to the park," said Matt. "Can **you**

_____ join **us** _____?"

"Can **we** _____ play with **your**

_____ ball?" asked Stephanie. "**Ours**

_____ is missing."

"**Yours** _____ is missing? That's too bad," said

Anna. "Sure, **you** _____ can play with **our**

_____ ball."

Matt, Anna, Andrew, and Stephanie all walked to the park. They would all play together.

"I'll throw the ball to you," said Matt to Andrew. Then you can throw the ball

to **them** _____," Matt said pointing to Anna and Stephanie.

"Hey," yelled Anna. "I see a ball ahead. Could it be Andrew and Stephanie's ball?"

"Yes, it could be **their**

_____

ball," answered Matt. Matt showed Andrew and Stephanie the ball. Sure enough, it was **theirs**

_____.

Lesson 1.5 Demonstrative Pronouns

A pronoun is a word used in place of a noun. Pronouns can be a subject, object, or possessive of the sentence. Pronouns can also be demonstrative.

Demonstrative pronouns replace nouns without naming the noun.
    this   that   these   those

> *This* is fun. (refers to an event or experience, for example a roller coaster)
> *That* was wonderful. (refers to an event or experience, for example a movie)
> *These* are good. (refers to a basket of apples)
> *Those* are better. (refers to a barrel of pears)

This and *these* are usually used when the person or object is closer to the writer and speaker. *That* and *those* are usually used when the person or object is farther away from the writer or speaker.

> *This* is fast (the roller coaster here), but *that* is faster (the roller coaster over there).
> *These* look good (the apples in the basket that is close), but *those look better* (the pears in the barrel across the room).

Demonstrative pronouns, like other pronouns, add variety to your writing and speaking.

Match It
Draw a line to match the demonstrative pronoun in Column A with the objects of the sentence in Column B.

Column A	Column B
this	many newspapers across the room
that	one magazine at the library
these	one wallet in a pocket
those	many pencils on the desk

---

this	many ants on the ground
that	one book on the shelf
these	many bananas at the store
those	one experience at a baseball game

Lesson 1.5 Demonstrative Pronouns

Proof It
Proof the following dialogue. Use the proofreading marks in the key to delete the demonstrative pronouns that are incorrect and insert the correct words.

> *e* - deletes incorrect word
> ^ - inserts correct word

Lauren and Devin like shopping at the mall. But sometimes they can be hard to please.

"Lauren, look at those!" (holding up earrings next to her ears)

Devin sighed, "I like this better." (pointing to earrings on a counter farther away)

"Maybe I don't want earrings at all," said Lauren. "What about these?" (waving her arm in the air to display a bracelet)

"No," said Devin. "Now, these is perfect!" (pointing to a belt hanging on the far wall)

"Devin, look at those. (pointing to a clock on the wall) I think the store is closing," cried Lauren.

"Yes, and these (pointing to the price tag on the belt) won't make my mom very happy," said Devin.

"Come on," replied Lauren. "Let's come back again tomorrow!"

Try It
Write more dialogue about Lauren and Devin's trip to the mall the next day. Be sure to use all four demonstrative pronouns: *this, that, these,* and *those.*

_____

_____

_____

_____

_____

_____

Lesson 1.6 Relative Pronouns

A pronoun is a word used in place of a noun. Pronouns can be the subject, the object, or the possessive of a sentence.

Relative pronouns are pronouns that are related to nouns that have already been stated. They combine two sentences that share a common noun.

who   whose   that   which

The woman, *who* is a doctor, wasn't at the party.
Who refers to the noun *woman*.

The parents, *whose* children were at the party, were ready to go.
Whose refers to the noun *parents*.
(This relative pronoun shows possession).

The note *that* you read is incorrect.
That refers to the noun *note*.

The newspaper articles, *which* are long, must be cut.
Which refers to the noun *newspaper articles*.

Complete It
Complete the following sentences by choosing the correct relative pronoun in parentheses. Circle the correct answer.

1. Someone (who, that) likes kiwi usually likes strawberries.

2. Bicyclers (which, whose) bikes are ready can go to the starting line.

3. He likes movies (which, that) have a lot of action.

4. The man, (who, whose) lives across the street, is an actor.

5. The car (who, that) you drove is blocking the driveway.

6. The bananas, (which, that) are the ripest, are used in the recipe.

Lesson 1.6 Relative Pronouns

Solve It
Solve the following riddle. Use a relative pronoun to fill in the blanks.

that	who
which	whose

Who bakes apple pies?

The man _____ grows apples bakes pies.

Who makes the best apple pies?

The man _____ apples are the sweetest bakes the best pies.

What didn't get baked into the pie?

The apple _____ had a bruise did not go in the pie.

What won the prize?

The pies, _____ were the sweetest, won the prize.

Try It
Try writing a riddle of your own. Follow the example above. Ask questions that require an answer with a relative pronoun. Use each relative pronoun at least once.

_____

_____

_____

_____

_____

_____

_____

_____

_____

_____

_____

_____

_____

_____

Lesson 1.7 Indefinite Pronouns

Indefinite pronouns are pronouns that do not specifically name the noun that comes before it (as do the relative pronouns).

all   another   any   anybody   anyone   anything   each   everybody
everyone   everything   few   many   nobody   none   one   several
some   somebody   someone

Many were invited to the party, but only a few came.
We donated *everything* from the attic to the charity foundation.
They looked everywhere for copies of the report, but found *none*.

Identify It
Underline the indefinite pronouns in the following paragraph.

The fair was approaching. Each of the cooks in town made ice cream cones for the fair. The cooks were put in pairs. One made the ice cream while another made the cones. You wouldn't think there would be any problems. However, there were some. One wanted the same flavor. Another wanted cherry. Someone wanted chocolate. Several even ate two scoops. That means someone had none. Everyone would think that is unfair. But the cooks were ready for anything. They made snow cones and everybody ate those instead. What else could happen? The sun melted the ice cream and the snow cones. Cooks quickly handed napkins to everyone with ice cream or snow cones. Then, they made milkshakes. Everything turned out fine.

Lesson 1.7 Indefinite Pronouns

Rewrite It

Rewrite the following school news report. Replace the underlined words with indefinite pronouns. More than one answer is acceptable in many sentences.

The whole community attended the fundraiser for the school. The bake sale was a big success. Not a single item was left at the end of the evening. Chris and his friends looked for more brownies. The whole Carson family went home with something. Most of the students enjoyed the food, music, and art. Almost all of the student art pieces were purchased. Six or seven of the attendees want to help with next year's fundraiser.

_____

_____

_____

_____

_____

_____

_____

_____

_____

Try It

Write a story about a recent gathering, like a family picnic or birthday party. Use at least eight indefinite pronouns. Underline each of them.

_____

_____

_____

_____

_____

_____

_____

_____

_____

_____

_____

Lesson 1.8 Verbs: Regular Present and Past Tense

A **verb** is a word that tells the action or the state of being of a sentence. In this sentence, *walk* is the verb. It tells the action of the sentence.

The students *walk* home.

In this sentence, *shared* is the verb. It tells the action of the sentence.

Kevin *shared* his cake with Carol at the party last night.

In the first sentence the action is taking place now. In the second sentence the action took place in the past. Add **ed** to the present tense of a **regular verb** to make it past tense. If the word already ends in the letter **e**, just add the letter **d**.

Complete It

Write each word in present tense in the first sentence and then in past tense in the second sentence.

1. act   Today, I _____.   Yesterday, I _____.

2. mend   Today, I _____.   Yesterday, I _____.

3. cook   Today, I _____.   Yesterday, I _____.

4. bake   Today, I _____.   Yesterday, I _____.

5. answer   Today, I _____.   Yesterday, I _____.

6. cycle   Today, I _____.   Yesterday, I _____.

7. wave   Today, I _____.   Yesterday, I _____.

8. scream   Today, I _____.   Yesterday, I _____.

9. bike   Today, I _____.   Yesterday, I _____.

10. jump   Today, I _____.   Yesterday, I _____.

11. mow   Today, I _____.   Yesterday, I _____.

12. yell   Today, I _____.   Yesterday, I _____.

13. rake   Today, I _____.   Yesterday, I _____.

14. whisper   Today, I _____.   Yesterday, I _____.

15. divide   Today, I _____.   Yesterday, I _____.

Lesson 1.8 Verbs: Regular Present and Past Tense

Proof It
Proofread the following announcement. Use the proofreading marks to correct mistakes with the present and past tense forms of verbs and insert the correctly spelled words. Not all of the verbs are from this lesson.

- *e* — deletes word
- ∧ — inserts word

Hello from Northland Auditorium, home of the Riverdale Cook-Off and Bake-Off. The chefs are ready for the bake-off. The chefs cook meals last night. The judges award prizes for the best meals last night. The chefs baked today. Early this morning, the judges call the chefs over. They talk with them about their recipes. The judges will now observed the baking. Judge Wilson and Judge Boggs looked over many of the cooks' shoulders. They laughed. It must be good news. I don't think they would joked if it weren't. Two cooks answered a question for the judges. They act nervous. The judges tasted all of the baked goods. What will win the blue ribbon? Will cookies, cakes, brownies, or candy captured the top prize? The judges now handed a note to the announcer. The winner is....

Try It
Write a first-hand account of a school event. Include both present and past tense regular verbs.

_____
_____
_____
_____
_____
_____
_____
_____

Lesson 1.10 Subject-Verb Agreement

Subject-verb agreement means verbs must agree in number with the subject of the sentence. If the subject is singular, then use a singular verb. If the subject is plural, use a plural verb.

The apple *tastes* good.   The apples *taste* good.
The flower *is* beautiful.   The flowers *are* beautiful.

If the subject is a compound subject, two subjects connected by the word *and*, then a plural verb is needed.

Tyler and Inez *bake* pies.   Tyler *bakes* pies.

If the subject is a compound subject connected by the words *or* or *nor*, then the verb will agree with the subject that is closer to the verb.

Neither Tyler **nor** Inez *likes* blueberry pie. (Inez likes)
Does Tyler **or** his brothers *like* banana cream pie? (brothers like)

If the subject and the verb are separated by a word or words, be sure that the verb still agrees with the subject.

Inez as well as her sisters *works* at the bakery.

Complete It
Circle the correct verb for each sentence.

1. Jill (jump, jumps) rope after school.

2. Jill and Katie (jump, jumps) rope after school.

3. Jill and her friends (jump, jumps) rope after school.

4. Jill as well as her friends (jump, jumps) rope after school.

5. Ross (like, likes) veggie lasagna.

6. Ross and Regina (like, likes) veggie lasagna.

7. Ross and his brothers (like, likes) veggie lasagna.

8. Ross as well as his parents (like, likes) veggie lasagna.

9. Does Jill or her friends (want, wants) to ride with me?

10. Neither Jill nor Katie (want, wants) to go to the movies.

Lesson 1.10 Subject-Verb Agreement

Rewrite It

Rewrite the following paragraph, correcting the subject-verb agreement mistakes as you go. Remember to be on the look out for subjects and verbs that are separated.

Sea turtles grows in many sizes and colors. They ranges between 100 and 1300 pounds. Instead of teeth, sea turtles has beaks in their jaws. Which of their senses is most keen? That would be their sense of smell. A female sea turtle lay her eggs on land. Unfortunately, sea turtles are in danger. But in the last 100 years, the population have become almost extinct. What can we do to ensure the survival of sea turtles? We can all helps by keeping our oceans clean. We can educate ourselves about the causes of habitat destruction. We can spread the word to others. Knowledge are a powerful tool in the world of our environment. The sea turtles is counting on us.

_____

_____

_____

_____

_____

_____

_____

_____

_____

_____

_____

_____

_____

Try It

Write a nonfiction paragraph about a reptile or insect that interests you. Underline the subjects of each sentence and circle the verbs.

_____

_____

_____

_____

_____

_____

Lesson 1.11 Action Verbs

Action verbs tell the action of the sentence. Action verbs come in both regular and irregular forms. They have present, past, and future tense forms, too.

Sandy and Karen *visit* every spring.
Sandy and Karen *visited* last year.
Sandy and Karen will *visit* next winter.

I bet Stan and Mike *eat* the whole apple pie.
I *ate* the whole apple.
I will *eat* the apple after I wash it.

Solve It

Look at the following pictures. On the line below each picture, write the action verb that the subject in the picture is doing.

1. _____

2. _____

3. _____

4. _____

5. _____

6. _____

Lesson 1.11   Action Verbs

Match It

One verb that is used very often in dialogue is *said*. Try to bring more variety to your writing by using other action verbs as a substitute for the verb *said*. Match the sentences in Column A with an action verb in Column B that could be substituted for the verb *said* in the sentence.

Column A	Column B
1. "Hey! We're over here!" said Marty _____	**a.** concluded
2. "I like taking walks at the park, too," said Kim. _____	**b.** began
3. "I promise it won't happen again," said Alex. _____	**c.** yelled
4. "Oh, I don't want to do more homework," said Justin. _____	**d.** reported
5. "We received 8 inches of snow over night," said the weather person. _____	**e.** added
6. "Those are the results of my survey," said the professor. _____	**f.** complained
7. "Be careful riding on the wet pavement," said Mom. _____	**g.** cautioned
8. "Would you like some more lemonade?" said the server. _____	**h.** groaned
9. "I don't like what's on my sandwich," said the customer. _____	**i.** vowed
10. "Let's start today's lesson," said the teacher. _____	**j.** asked

Try It

Write a letter to a friend or relative. Tell him or her about a recent event in school or another activity in which you participated. Use at least 10 action verbs. Underline the verbs in your letter.

_____

_____

_____

_____

_____

_____

_____

_____

_____

_____

Lesson 1.12 Helping Verbs

Helping verbs are not main verbs. They help to form some of the tenses of the main verbs. Helping verbs express time and mood.

shall	may	would	has	can
will	have	should	do	did
could	had	must		

The forms of the verb *to be* are also helping verbs:

is	are	was	were	am	been

Verbs ending in **ing** can be a clue that there is a helping verb in the sentence. Sometimes, there is more than one helping verb in a sentence. This is called a **verb phrase**.

The Olympic star *would practice* for hours.
The Olympic star *was practicing* for hours and hours.
The Olympic star *had been practicing* for hours and hours.

Complete It

Choose a helping verb or verb phrase from the box to complete each sentence. Underline the main verb of the sentence that it helps. The main verb does not always directly follow the helping verb. Sometimes there is another word in between. Some sentences can have more than one answer.

have had	has could	should would	must can	shall had been

1. _____ we dance to this song?

2. That _____ be the right direction, but I'm not sure.

3. Rick and Dana _____ waiting for hours when they finally got in.

4. _____ you go with me to the movies?

5. The children _____ go with their older brothers.

6. I _____ been a fan of hers for years.

7. It _____ been days since we've seen each other.

8. We _____ take this train; it will get us home faster.

9. It _____ be this way, I see a familiar house.

10. This assignment _____ taken a long time to finish.

Lesson 1.12 Helping Verbs

Proof It
Some of the sentences in the paragraph need helping verbs to make them complete. Insert helping verbs when needed.

^ - inserts words

Glacier National Park

Glacier National Park located in Montana. Glacier National Park aptly named. Glaciers left from the ice age remain in the park. Grizzly bears said to be the mascot of the park. Rangers said that they observed the bears' almost human-like behavior. The mountain goats of Glacier National Park live high in the mountains. The visitors go high up to find them. Glacier National Park known as one of the top night spots of the national parks. Because it is located far away from cities, the skies are dark and millions of stars seen at night. You visit Glacier National Park any time of year.

Try It
Write a nonfiction paragraph about a historical place. Use at least ten helping verbs or verb phrases.

_____

_____

_____

_____

_____

_____

_____

_____

_____

_____

Lesson 1.13 Linking Verbs

Linking verbs connect a subject to a noun or adjective. They do not express an action.

The most common linking verbs are the forms of the verb *to be:*

      is   are   was   were   been   am

Other linking verbs are those of the five senses:

      smell   look   taste   feel   sound

Other linking verbs reflect a state of being:

      appear   seem   become   grow   remain

A verb or adjective will follow these linking verbs in the sentence.

Identify It
Circle the linking verb and underline the noun or adjective that is linked in each sentence.

1. The crowd appears excited.
2. The crowd thought the play was good.
3. The lettuce tastes bitter.
4. The line seems long.
5. Syd, Mitzi, and Deb were runners.
6. Mr. Thomas became successful after much hard work.
7. The runners feel great running in the fresh air.
8. The lights grew dim as the play began.
9. The singer's voice sounds weak compared to the others.
10. Her future remains uncertain.
11. It has been a long day.
12. Dinner sounds great.
13. They are late.
14. I am hungry.
15. The snack is tasty.

Lesson 1.13 Linking Verbs

Rewrite It

Rewrite the paragraph, replacing the underlined helping verbs with linking verbs. Use the lists of linking verbs on page 30 if you need help.

    Don and Tina spent Saturday afternoon at the museum. The paintings <u>were</u> thought-provoking the longer they looked at them. The sculptures <u>were</u> tasteful. The artifacts <u>were</u> fascinating. The rooms <u>were</u> quiet as they walked through each one. They stopped for a snack at the café. The coffee <u>was</u> wonderful. The muffins <u>were</u> delicious. They stopped at the gift shop before they left the museum. The post cards of some of the paintings <u>were</u> perfect for Don's nieces. Don and Tina enjoyed the afternoon. At the end of the day, they <u>were</u> tired and were ready to go home. However, the museum <u>is</u> one of their favorite places to visit. They <u>are</u> special when they go.

_____

_____

_____

_____

_____

_____

_____

_____

_____

_____

_____

_____

Try It

Write a paragraph about a place you like to visit. Give information and details about this place. Use at least five linking verbs in your paragraph.

_____

_____

_____

_____

_____

_____

_____

Lesson 1.14 Transitive Verbs

Transitive verbs transfer their action to a direct or indirect object. If the object doesn't receive the action of the verb, the meaning of the verb is not complete.

> The hail storm *broke* the *car windows.*
> Transitive Verb = broke
> Object = car windows (what was broke)

The meaning of the verb *broke* would not be complete without the object *car windows.*

The object and receiver of a transitive verb can be either a direct object or an indirect object.

A direct object receives the action directly from the subject.

> They *sent* a *claim.*
> Transitive Verb = sent
> Direct Object = claim (what was sent)

An indirect object is the person to whom or for whom the action is directed.

> They *sent the insurance agency* a *claim.*
> Transitive Verb = sent
> Direct Object = claim (what was sent)
> Indirect Object = the insurance agency (to whom the claim was sent)

Match It

The partial sentence in Column B completes the sentence started in Column A. Column A contains the subjects of the sentences and the transitive verbs. Column B contains the direct and indirect objects. Draw a line from Column A to the sentence ending that makes the most sense in Column B.

<u>Column A</u>	<u>Column B</u>
1. Karen's father bought	his fans a story.
2. The outfielder caught	the ice cubes for later.
3. The artist drew	a picture.
4. The boys drank	the ball.
5. The teacher gave	soy beans and pumpkins.
6. The team ate	several pizzas.
7. The swimmers swam	many laps.
8. The farmer grew	them gold stars.
9. The author wrote	her a present.
10. Marie froze	the lemonade.

Lesson 1.14 Transitive Verbs

Rewrite It

Now that you have connected the sentences in Column A and Column B, rewrite them on the following lines. Then, circle the transitive verbs, underline the direct objects, and double underline the indirect objects.

_____

_____

_____

_____

_____

_____

_____

_____

_____

_____

_____

_____

_____

_____

Try It

Choose eight of the transitive verbs used in this lesson and write sentences of your own. Be sure to include a direct object. Two sentences should use indirect objects.

_____

_____

_____

_____

_____

_____

_____

Lesson 1.15 Gerunds, Participles, and Infinitives

Gerunds, **participles**, and **infinitives** are other kinds of verbs. These verbs take the role of another part of speech in some circumstances.

A **gerund** is when a verb is used as a noun. A verb can take the form of the noun when the ending **-ing** is added.

> *Cooking* is one of my favorite activities.
> (The subject *cooking* is a noun in the sentence.)

A **participle** is when a verb is used as an adjective. A verb can take the form of an adjective when the endings **-ing** or **-ed** are added.

> Those *falling* snowflakes from the sky are pretty.
> (*falling* modifies *snowflakes*)
> The *ordered* parts should be here on Monday.
> (*ordered* modifies *parts*)

An **infinitive** is when a verb is used as a noun, adjective, or adverb. A verb can take the form of a noun, adjective, or adverb when preceded by the word *to*.

> *To agree* with the professor can be important.
> (The verb *to agree* acts as the subject, noun, of the sentence.)
> The last student *to report* on the subject led the research team.
> (The verb *to report* acts as an adjective modifying *student*.)
> Roger observed the long movie *to report* on it for the paper.
> (The verb *to report* acts as an adverb modifying *observed*.)

Complete It
Choose a verb from the box to fill in the blanks in the sentences.

to catch	joking	sleeping
to drink	reported	to warn

1. _____ is Jed's favorite activity on the weekends.

2. She jumped high _____ the ball.

3. The _____ comedians performed at school.

4. Jim takes plenty of water _____ on long runs.

5. The _____ details of the event were surprising.

6. _____ the public of the oncoming storm was her job.

Lesson 1.15 Gerunds, Participles, and Infinitives

Identify It

The following sentences contain verbs that are acting as gerunds, participles, or infinitives. Identify which by placing a **G** for gerund, a **P** for participle, or an **I** for infinitive after each sentence. Then, underline the gerund, participle, or infinitive.

1. Acting is all Sally wants to do. _____

2. The students singing on stage are from our school. _____

3. Logs burned in this fireplace are small. _____

4. To jump for the shot would be the best thing to do. _____

5. Matthew brought a sandwich to eat in case the meeting ran long. _____

6. Ann watched the special on television to learn about habitats. _____

7. Amy studied the styles of ancient Rome to sew the appropriate costume. _____

8. Running is an excellent exercise. _____

9. Karen brings sweaters to wear in case it gets cold at night. _____

10. The sound of children laughing is a wonderful sound. _____

11. To shake a broken VCR is not a good idea. _____

12. The polished car sparkled in the sunlight. _____

Try It

Make a list of six verbs. Write them on the lines below. Then, change them to gerunds, participles, and infinitives and use them in sentences. Write your new sentences on the lines provided.

_____   _____   _____

_____   _____   _____

_____

_____

_____

_____

_____

Lesson 1.16 Adjectives

Adjectives are words used to describe a noun or pronoun. Most adjectives are common adjectives. Common adjectives are not proper, so they are not capitalized.

> The *cold* water felt good on the *hot* day.
> *Water* and *day* are the nouns. The adjectives *cold* and *hot* describe the nouns.

Proper adjectives are formed from proper nouns and are always capitalized.

> The children wanted snow cones and *French* fries at the amusement park.
> The proper adjective *French* describes the noun, *fries*.

Solve It

The words in the box are adjectives of the senses. Find and circle these words in the puzzle. They can be horizontal, vertical, diagonal, forward, and backward.

bright	loud	fresh	sour	cool
dim	sharp	sweet	spicy	rough
pretty	soothing	woodsy	tart	soft

b	m	s	u	y	t	t	e	r	p
r	c	n	o	c	f	o	h	t	t
i	k	g	e	i	r	r	f	n	w
g	p	e	n	m	e	o	b	b	y
h	r	b	u	i	s	w	e	e	t
t	a	r	t	d	h	n	c	g	y
e	h	o	r	u	e	t	o	b	c
n	s	u	z	o	z	g	o	i	i
u	o	g	g	l	e	r	l	o	p
s	a	h	w	o	o	d	s	y	s

Lesson 1.16 Adjectives

Identify It
Circle the common adjectives and underline the proper adjectives in the paragraph.

Marblehead Lighthouse

Lighthouses are tall towers with bright lights that guide ships at night or in the fog. One famous lighthouse is located in Marblehead, Ohio, on Lake Erie. It is one of Lake Erie's most-photographed landmarks. Marblehead Lighthouse is the oldest lighthouse in continuous operation on the Great Lakes. It has been in operation since 1822. The 65-foot high tower is made of limestone. Throughout the years, the lighthouse has been operated by 15 lighthouse keepers. Two of the 15 keepers were women. Lighthouse keepers had many duties. They lighted the projection lamps, kept logs of passing ships, recorded the weather, and organized rescue efforts. As technology changed with time, the type of light used also changed. Electric light replaced lanterns in 1923. Today a 300mm lens flashes green signals every six seconds. It can be seen for up to 11 nautical miles. The lighthouse no longer has a resident keeper. The United States Coast Guard now operates the Marblehead Lighthouse. The lighthouse beacon continues to warn sailors and keep those on the lake waters safe.

Try It
Choose 10 of the 15 sensory adjectives from the puzzle on page 36. Use each of the 10 adjectives in a sentence.

_____

_____

_____

_____

_____

_____

_____

_____

_____

_____

Lesson 1.17 Adverbs

Adverbs are words used to modify a verb, an adjective, or another adverb.

An adverb tells *how, why, when, where, how often*, and *how much*.

Adverbs often end in **ly** (but not always).
    how or *why*: softly, courageously, forcefully
    when or *how often*: sometimes, yesterday, always
    where: here, inside, below
    how much: generously, barely, liberally

Match It
The categories in Column A are missing their adverbs. Select adverbs from Column B and write them in the appropriate category in Column A.

Column A	Column B
Category 1: *how or why*	scarcely
_____	today
_____	cleverly
_____	outside
	joyfully
Category 2: *when or how often*	entirely
_____	there
_____	tomorrow
_____	never
	luckily
Category 3: *where*	wholly
_____	up
_____	
_____	
Category 4: *how much*	
_____	
_____	
_____	

Lesson 1.17 Adverbs

Identify It
Circle the adverbs in the following paragraphs. Underline the verbs, adjectives, or adverbs they modify.

An All-American Hero

Jesse Owens lived from 1913-1980. He didn't have much money growing up, but he had ambition. He worked tirelessly at part-time jobs to help support his family. His high school coach noticed Jesse's talent for running. Because of work, Jesse couldn't practice with the team after school. He graciously accepted his coach's offer to train in the morning.

Jesse was anxiously recruited by many colleges and accepted an offer to the Ohio State University. However, since he was African American, he received no scholarships, despite the fact that he broke several world records while attending OSU. He continued to energetically work, study, and train. In the Berlin Olympic Games in 1936, he became the first American to win four gold medals in a single game. He also broke many track records. Remarkably, his records lasted more than 20 years.

What is even more remarkably significant is his dedication to the well-being of others that he actively exhibited later in life. He became a spokesman for living a life guided by hard work and loyalty. He eagerly sponsored and participated in youth sports programs in underprivileged neighborhoods. After his death in 1980, his wife continued to operate the Jesse Owens Foundation. Jesse Owens truly deserved the Medal of Freedom he was awarded in 1976. It is the highest honor a United States civilian can receive.

Try It
Write a sentence for each adverb in the verb box. Be sure your adverbs modify verbs, adjectives, or other adverbs.

actively	energetically
after	several
anxiously	tirelessly

_____

_____

_____

_____

_____

_____

Lesson 1.18 Conjunctions

Conjunctions connect individual words or groups of words in sentences. There are three types of conjunctions.

Coordinate conjunctions connect words, phrases, or independent clauses that are equal or of the same type. Coordinate conjunctions are *and, but, or, nor, for,* and *yet.*
> The horse's mane is soft *and* shiny.

Correlative conjunctions are used with pairs and are used together. *Both/and, either/or,* and *neither/nor* are examples of correlative conjunctions.
> *Neither* pizza *nor* pasta was listed on the menu.

Subordinate conjunctions connect two clauses that are not equal. They connect dependent clauses to independent clauses in order to complete the meaning. *After, as long as, since,* and *while* are examples of subordinate conjunctions.
> We can't save for our spring vacation *until* we get part time jobs.

Match It

Match the words in Column A with their relationship in Column B.

Column A	Column B
1. provided that the light is green	equal (coordinate)
2. cold and fluffy snow	pairs (correlative)
3. either smooth or crunchy	dependent (subordinate)

4. both mushrooms and olives	equal (coordinate)
5. before it gets dark	pairs (correlative)
6. purple or blue shirt	dependent (subordinate)

7. after the race	equal (coordinate)
8. neither pennies nor nickels	pairs (correlative)
9. music and dance	dependent (subordinate)

Lesson 1.18 Conjunctions

Identify It

Identify whether the following sentences use coordinate, correlative, or subordinate conjunctions by writing a **CD** for coordinate, **CR** for correlative, or **S** for subordinate before each sentence. Then, underline the conjunctions.

1. _____ Bobcats, members of the lynx family, are found in North America and Northern Eurasia.

2. _____ Although they are members of the lynx family, they differ in a number of ways.

3. _____ Bobcats have smaller ear tufts and feet than lynxes.

4. _____ Because of the terrain bobcats can have different body types.

5. _____ Bobcats living in northern territories are smaller and have pale coats.

6. _____ Bobcats living in southern territories are larger and have dark coats.

7. _____ Bobcats can be found in swampy areas but also desert areas.

8. _____ Bobcats hunt both during the night and during the day.

9. _____ Though smaller in size, bobcats are more aggressive than lynxes.

10. _____ Bobcats can climb and swim well.

11. _____ Not only bobcats but all big cats are exploited for their fur.

12. _____ Because of this and other threats to the cat family, conservation groups are working to halt species extinction.

Try It

Write six sentences that use conjunctions. Write two sentences using coordinate conjunctions, two sentences using correlative conjunctions, and two sentences using subordinate conjunctions.

_____

_____

_____

_____

_____

_____

_____

_____

Lesson 1.19 Interjections

An **interjection** is a word or phrase used to express surprise or strong emotion.

Common interjections include: ah; alas; aw; cheers; eeek; eh; hey; hi; huh; hurray; oh; oh, no; ouch; uh; uh-huh; uh-uh; voila; wow; yeah

Exclamation marks are usually used after interjections to separate them from the rest of the sentence.

Hurray! We are the champions!

If the feeling isn't quite as strong, a comma is used in place of the exclamation point.

Yeah, the Oakdale Grizzlies had a great basketball season!

Sometimes question marks are used as an interjection's punctuation.

Well? How does the team look for next year?

Solve It

What interjection from the above list would you choose to add to the following sentences? Use the pictures to help you decide. Write them on the blank in the sentences.

1. _____ It's so good to see you.

2. _____ We've made it to the top.

3. _____ I really scraped up my knee!

4. _____ Tonight we celebrate!

5. _____ Dessert is served.

6. _____ I hope I do better on the next test.

Lesson 1.19 Interjections

Rewrite It

Rewrite the following dialogue. Add interjections where you think they are appropriate to make the dialogue more exciting and interesting. Choose interjections from the previous page, or add some of your own.

"We're about ready to land. Look at that landscape," exclaimed Dana as the plane made its descent at the Kona International Airport on the big island, Hawaii. The guide book says this airport sits on miles of lava rock."

"How can that be?" asked Gabriella.

"There are five volcanoes on Hawaii. One is extinct, one is dormant, and three are still active," answered Dana.

"There are active volcanoes here?" uttered Gabriella.

"The one that caused the lava flow beneath this airport is Hualalai," reported Dana. "It is still considered active. In the 1700s, it spewed lava all the way to the ocean. The airport is on top of one of the flows. The world's largest volcano, Mauna Loa, and the world's most active volcano, Kilauea, are also here on Hawaii."

"Dana, are you sure you want to vacation on this island?" asked Gabriella.

"I plan to visit all of the volcanoes," answered Dana.

"I'm hitting the beach. I've got some serious surfing to do!" exclaimed Gabriella.

_____

_____

_____

_____

_____

_____

_____

_____

_____

_____

_____

_____

_____

_____

NAME _____

Lesson 1.20 Prepositions

Prepositions are words or groups of words that show the relationship between a noun or pronoun (the object of the sentence) and another word in the sentence.

They sat *upon the dock.*

In this sentence, *upon* is the preposition, and *dock* is the object of the preposition.

Common prepositions:

above	below	in	under
across	beneath	inside	until
after	beside	into	up
along	between	near	with
around	by	off	within
at	down	on	without
away	during	outside	
because	except	over	
before	for	to	
behind	from	toward	

Complete It

Complete the following sentences by circling the preposition that works best in the sentence.

1. Look (behind, down from) your car before you back out.

2. I really like the little café right (across, away from) the street.

3. The kitty likes watching the birds (outside, toward) the window.

4. Our cats only live (around, inside).

5. Edna stored the photographs (through, underneath) her bed.

6. Cedric can't go on the field trip (within, without) his permission slip.

7. The commentators predicted the outcome of the game (before, until) it was over.

8. The snow piled (on top of, over to) the ice.

Lesson 1.20 Prepositions

Identify It
Circle the prepositions and underline the objects of the prepositions in the paragraph.

What Is the West Wing?

The West Wing is located in the White House. The President of the United States has his office in the West Wing. It is called the Oval Office. The West Wing houses the executive staff's offices, in addition to the President's office. The chief of staff's office is across from the Oval Office. The vice president works beside the chief of staff. The press secretary and the communication director's offices are along the main corridor. The Roosevelt Room (a conference room), the Cabinet Room (the cabinet is a group of advisers who are heads of government departments), and the President's secretary's office are a little farther down the corridor. Outside of the press secretary's window is the Rose Garden. The West Colonnade runs alongside the Rose Garden. The Press Room is inside the West Colonnade. The Press Room sits on top of an old swimming pool. The swimming pool is a remnant of Franklin D. Roosevelt's administration. That completes the tour of the West Wing.

Try It
Write a paragraph describing the rooms in your home. Tell where the rooms are located and what sits outside of some of the windows. Circle the prepositions you used.

_____

_____

_____

_____

_____

_____

_____

_____

_____

_____

_____

_____

Lesson 1.21 Prepositional Phrases

Prepositional phrases include the prepositions and the objects (nouns or pronouns) that follow the prepositions. A prepositional phrase includes the preposition, the object of the preposition, and the modifiers (describes other words) of the object. Prepositional phrases tell about *when* or *where* something is happening.

They sat *upon the dock*.

If the noun in the prepositional phrase above had modifiers, they would also be included in the prepositional phrase.

They sat *upon the wooden dock*.

Match It

Match the beginnings of sentences in Column A with the prepositional phrases that match them best in Column B.

Column A	Column B
1. The clouds are	within the limits.
2. We can leave now	in the sky.
3. Let's have dinner	after the movie.
4. The lake lies far	in her place.
5. When alphabetizing the files, put the As	outside the window.
6. Annie can't baby sit, so Laurie is coming	in front of the Bs.
7. It was raining so hard it was difficult to see	since the babysitter is here.
8. Swimming is permitted if you stay	beyond the forest.

Lesson 1.21 Prepositional Phrases

Solve It

The following sentences describe the above scene. However, the prepositions are missing. Look at the picture and complete the sentences.

1. The kids played _____ the fence.

2. A cat looked _____ a window.

3. A squirrel sat _____ the roof.

4. Chimney smoke rose _____ the house.

5. The basement was _____ the house.

6. The clouds floated _____ the sky.

7. The tree sat _____ the fence.

8. A jogger ran _____ the street.

Try It

Write four sentences that include prepositional phrases. Underline the prepositional phrases in your sentences.

_____

_____

_____

_____

Lesson 1.22 Articles

Articles are specific words that serve as adjectives before a noun. *A*, *an*, and *the* are articles.

The is a **definite article**. That means it names a specific noun.

I go to *the* school on *the* corner.

The article *the* tells that the person goes to a specific school on a specific corner.

A and *an* are **indefinite articles**. They do not name a specific noun.

I would like to go to *a* school on *a* corner.

The article *a* tells that the person wants to go to a school on a corner, but not a specific school or corner.

Use *a* when the noun it precedes begins with a consonant or a vowel that sounds like a consonant.

a dog   a cat   a skunk   a one-way street

Use *an* when the noun it precedes begins with a vowel or sounds like it starts with a vowel.

an envelope   an olive   an island   an honest person

Complete It

Complete the following sentences by circling the correct answer in parentheses.

1. Mike and Jen rented the apartment above (a, an, the) bookstore.

2. Henry wants to get (a, an, the) car with four doors.

3. An amoeba is (a, an, the) one-celled animal.

4. Coordinating the play turned out to be quite (a, an, the) ordeal.

5. Todd wants to rent (a, an, the) canoe for the weekend.

6. Kay brought (a, an, the) orange to go with her lunch.

7. (A, An, The) orange sweater looked best on Karley.

8. Not (a, an, the) hour went by that they didn't think about each other.

9. (A, An, The) Kensington Trail is beautiful.

10. Lynn wants to buy (a, an, the) blue or red bracelet.

Lesson 1.22 Articles

Proof It
Proofread the following paragraph. Change any incorrect articles to the correct ones.

> *e* – deletes incorrect letters, words, punctuation
> ^ – inserts correct letters, words, punctuation

The Tonys

Almost everyone has heard of the Oscars, an Emmys, and a Golden Globe Awards. The Tony Awards is also a awards presentation. A Tony Awards are given for outstanding accomplishment in theater. The Tony Awards were named after Antoinette Perry, a actress, director, producer, and manager. She was known for helping young people who were interested in the acting profession. An first Tony Awards were presented in 1947 with seven categories. Today, there are 25 categories including Best Play and Best Musical. The Tony award is the medallion that shows a image of Antoinette Perry on one side. On an other side are a masks of comedy and tragedy.

Try It
What is your favorite play, movie, or television show? Write a paragraph describing your favorite. Underline the articles you used.

_____

_____

_____

_____

_____

_____

_____

_____

_____

_____

Review Chapter 1 Lessons 1–22

Review: Common and Proper Nouns; Regular Plural Nouns; Irregular Plural Nouns; Personal Pronouns; Demonstrative Pronouns; Relative Pronouns; Indefinite Pronouns

Putting It Together
Complete the following sentences by circling the best answer in parentheses.

1. I like to visit the (museum, Museum) on Sundays.

2. The New York (museum, Museum) of Art is one famous museum.

3. Paul Klee was a famous artist who loved and painted many (cats, cat).

4. (Women, Womans) were the subject of many of the paintings of Henri Matisse.

5. Claude Monet's parents did not want (he, him) to become an artist.

6. But (that, those) didn't stop him.

7. Marc Chagall liked to paint violins in memory of his uncle (which, who) played.

8. The impressionist artist Pierre-Auguste Renoir believed (anyone, everyone) should work with their hands.

Review: Verbs: Regular Present and Past Tense; Verbs: Irregular Present and Past Tense; Subject-Verb Agreement; Action Verbs; Helping Verbs; Linking Verbs; Transitive Verbs; Gerunds, Participles, Infinitives

Circle the regular past tense verb and underline the irregular past tense verb.

1. Last weekend we played ball and we built sand castles.

Circle the action verb and underline the helping verb phrase.

2. The golfer hit the ball to the left; he should have hit it straight ahead.

Circle the transitive verb and underline its object.

3. The artists drew many paintings.

Circle the infinitive.

4. The author is going to write at the beach.

Review Chapter I Lessons I-22

Review: Adjectives; Adverbs; Conjunctions; Interjections; Prepositions; Prepositional Phrases; Articles

Identify adjectives (**ADJ**), adverbs (**ADV**), conjunctions (**C**), prepositions (**P**), and articles (**A**) in the following biography. Write the abbreviation on the line next to the word.

Leonardo da Vinci

One of _____ the greatest _____ artists of all time was more than just an _____ artist. He was a sculptor, scientist, inventor, engineer, astronomer, architect, musician, philosopher, and _____ mathematician. Leonardo da Vinci (1452–1519) was born in _____ Vinci, Italy. Da Vinci was a _____ genius. During his lifetime, he sketched objects that were ahead of _____ his time: the _____ airplane, the tank, and _____ the submarine. Da Vinci brilliantly _____ and beautifully _____ painted the human _____ body and other natural _____ objects. He was also a humanitarian.

Born during _____ the Renaissance, the _____ period in history that represented the great _____ rebirth of art, literature, and learning in 14th, 15th, and 16th century Europe, da Vinci became known as the perfect _____ example of _____ the Renaissance _____ Man. Leonardo da Vinci painted the famous _____ *Mona Lisa* and _____ *The Last Supper*, both of which now hang in _____ The Louvre in Paris, France.

Lesson 1.23 Declarative Sentences

Declarative sentences are sentences that make statements. They say something about a place, person, thing, or idea. When punctuating a declarative sentence, use a period at the end.

I have several hours of homework to do.

Identify It

Identify the following declarative sentences by placing a checkmark ✓ on the line provided. Leave the other sentences blank.

1. _____ Have you ever heard of a red-eyed tree frog?

2. _____ Red-eyed tree frogs are small, colorful, musical frogs with big red eyes.

3. _____ Where do red-eyed tree frogs live?

4. _____ They primarily live in South America, Central America, and parts of Mexico.

5. _____ They like lowland rainforests close to rivers and hills.

6. _____ How small are red-eyed tree frogs?

7. _____ Female red-eyed tree frogs grow to be 3 inches long.

8. _____ Males grow to be only 2 inches long.

9. _____ Do they have any color other than red eyes?

10. _____ Their bodies are neon green with dashes of yellow and blue.

11. _____ Their upper legs are bright blue and their feet are orange or red.

12. _____ How are these tree frogs musical?

13. _____ Red-eyed tree frogs are nocturnal and can be heard in their trees at night.

14. _____ Why are these frogs called *tree frogs*?

15. _____ They live mostly in trees.

Lesson 1.23 Declarative Sentences

Proof It

Proofread the following journal entry. Some of the periods have been left off. Add periods where they are needed using the proofreading mark.

⊙ **– inserts period**

Saturday, May 6

Dear Diary,

Something amazing happened today I am going to be in a movie. The movie, *The Time Travelers,* is being filmed in my town. My mom works at the library. The director was learning about the history of the town at the library My mom helped the director find what she needed. The director saw my picture on my mom's desk She asked my mom if I would be interested in a small part in the movie. Would I ever!

I will have only two lines to say Mom said she will help me memorize them. My scene will last about five minutes. Do you know what the best part is? I get to work with two of my favorite actors of all time I can't wait to start filming. Who knows? Maybe I'll be famous one day

Try It

Write four declarative sentences about a subject of your choosing. Don't forget to use periods at the end of your sentences.

1. _____

2. _____

3. _____

4. _____

Lesson 1.24 Interrogative Sentences

Interrogative sentences are sentences that ask questions. When punctuating an interrogative sentence, use a question mark.

Do you live in the country or in the city**?**

Complete It

Complete the following sentences by circling the correct punctuation at the end of the sentences.

1. Who is your hero (? .)
2. Do you have Mr. Bell for history this year (? .)
3. What is your favorite food (? .)
4. Can we leave first thing in the morning (? .)
5. When does the bus leave (? .)
6. Green is my favorite color (? .)
7. Where are we going on the field trip next week (? .)
8. I'm going to have Mr. Stubbert for history next year (? .)
9. Why don't we go out for dinner (? .)
10. Can Charlie come over for dinner (? .)
11. How many stars are in the sky (? .)
12. I'm going to take the bus downtown (? .)
13. What's your favorite color (? .)
14. How many sisters and brothers do you have (? .)
15. Look at that unusual building (? .)
16. Have you ever seen the Grand Canyon (? .)
17. Are you going to take swimming lessons this summer (? .)
18. I am so clumsy, I dropped my tray at lunch (? .)
19. How do you want to decorate the gym for the dance (? .)
20. I like broccoli on my salad (? .)

Lesson 1.24 Interrogative Sentences

Complete It
Complete the following notes a reporter made about the upcoming Iditarod race by adding periods and question marks where they are needed.

Story

The Iditarod

Notes

What is the Iditarod The Iditarod is a sled dog race

Where and when is the Iditarod held The Iditarod is held in Alaska in March. It starts in Anchorage and finishes in Nome

What is the distance of the race The race covers 1,049 miles

Who participates in the Iditarod The sleds are led by men and women called mushers Twelve to eighteen dogs pull the sleds

What is the training like for the Iditarod Training for the Iditarod is challenging for the mushers and the dogs Dogs run approximately 1,500 miles in training each year

Who takes care of the dogs Mushers take good care of their dogs Veterinarians and volunteers help along the course

What was the best finishing time in an Iditarod The best finishing time was 9 days, 2 hours, 42 minutes, and 19 seconds by Doug Swingley in 1995

Try It
Who? What? When? Where? Why? How? These are the questions reporters ask when they are investigating a story. Chose an event, and write down the questions you would ask if you were a reporter. Don't forget to use question marks at the end of your interrogative sentences.

Event: _____

Questions: _____

_____

_____

_____

_____

_____

_____

Lesson 1.25 Exclamatory Sentences

Exclamatory sentences are sentences that reveal urgency, strong surprise, or emotion. When punctuating an exclamatory sentence, use an exclamation mark.

> Watch out for the icy steps!

Sometimes you will find interjections in exclamatory sentences.

> *Yea!* One more test until summer break!

Exclamation marks can also be used in dialogue, when the character or speaker is making an urgent or emotional statement.

> "*Watch out!*" shouted Kelly.

Exclamation marks should be used sparingly in writing. Do not overuse them.

Match It

Match the sentences (which are missing their punctuation) in Column A with their type of sentence in Column B. Draw an arrow to make your match.

Column A	Column B
1. I will be thirteen on my next birthday	declarative
2. Hurry and open up your presents	interrogative
3. How old are you	exclamatory

4. Oh no I dropped all of my papers in a puddle	declarative
5. Is it supposed to snow all weekend	interrogative
6. Autumn is my favorite season	exclamatory

7. Where are my shoes	declarative
8. I scored 12 points in the basketball game	interrogative
9. Look out	exclamatory

Lesson 1.25 Exclamatory Sentences

Proof It
Proofread the following skit. Add periods, question marks, or exclamation marks on the spaces.

"Karen and Dave," shouted Sandra, "we're going to a planetarium__"

"What is a planetarium__" questioned Karen.

"A planetarium," answered Sandra, "is a room with a large dome ceiling__ Images of the sky are projected onto the ceiling with a star projector."

Dave continued, "You can see the movements of the sun, moon, planets, and stars__ I've always wanted to go to a planetarium__"

Sandra said, "They shorten the time so you can see in just minutes what it takes the objects years to complete__"

"Will we be able to see the constellations of the zodiac__" asked Karen.

"Yes, I believe so," answered Dave. "We will even be able to see how the objects in the sky will look thousands of years from now__"

"We'll sit in seats like we're at the movie theater, but it will really look like we're outside," said Sandra.

Karen exclaimed, "I can't wait to go to the planetarium__"

Try It
Write four sentence pairs. Write four declarative sentences using periods as the end punctuation. Then, write four similar sentences that show stronger emotion or surprise. You can add interjections if you like. Be sure to change the end punctuation to an exclamation mark.

Declarative Sentences

1. _____

2. _____

3. _____

4. _____

Exclamatory Sentences

1. _____

2. _____

3. _____

4. _____

Lesson 1.27 Simple Sentences

Simple sentences are sentences with one independent clause. **Independent clauses** present a complete thought and can stand alone as a sentence. Simple sentences do not have any dependent clauses. **Dependent clauses** do not present a complete thought and cannot stand alone as sentences.

Simple sentences can have one or more subjects.
> *Goats* lived at the sanctuary.
> *Goats* and *turkeys* lived at the sanctuary.

Simple sentences can have one or more predicates.
> The goats *played* with the other animals.
> The turkeys *played* and *talked* with the other animals.

Simple sentences can have more than one subject and more than one predicate.
> The *goats* and the *turkeys played* and *talked* with the other animals.

Match It
Each of the simple sentences in Column A has select words underlined. The parts of speech that match the underlined words are found in Column B. Match the sentences in Column A with the parts of speech in Column B.

Column A

1. Farm Sanctuary <u>rescues</u> and <u>protects</u> farm animals.

2. <u>Farm Sanctuary members</u> have helped to pass farm animal protection laws.

3. The <u>New York sanctuary</u> and the <u>California sanctuary</u> are home to hundreds of rescued farm animals.

4. Farm Sanctuary <u>offers</u> a humane education program to schools.

5. At Farm Sanctuary, <u>people</u> and <u>animals</u> <u>work</u> and <u>play</u> together.

Column B

one subject

two subjects

one predicate

two predicates

two subjects/two predicates

Lesson 1.27 Simple Sentences

Identify It
Identify the subjects and predicates in the following simple sentences from a paragraph from a travel brochure. Circle the subject and underline the predicate of each sentence.

Hike, Bike, See Amazing Wildlife

You can experience the great outdoors at Acadia National Park in Maine. Many visitors hike and bike the miles of trails. Some trails have moderate to difficult climbs. More than 225 types of birds live in Acadia. Songbirds are popular in the spring. The winter brings the chickadees. Eagles, peregrine falcons, and ospreys inhabit Acadia. Perhaps the most famous birds are the Atlantic Puffins. Maine is the only place in the United States where puffins breed. Visitors who canoe and kayak can see puffins from the nearby bay. You can also take a specifically designed Puffin Cruise. You shouldn't miss the beauty of America's first national park east of the Mississippi.

Try It
Write the simple sentences as noted below.

1. one subject

   _____

2. more than one subject

   _____

   _____

3. one predicate

   _____

   _____

4. more than one predicate

   _____

   _____

5. more than one subject and more than one predicate

   _____

   _____

Lesson 1.28 Compound Sentences

Compound sentences are sentences with two or more simple sentences (independent clauses) joined by a coordinate conjunction, punctuation, or both. As in simple sentences, there are no dependent clauses in compound sentences.

A compound sentence can be two sentences joined with a comma and a coordinate conjunction.

> He didn't think he was a fan of Shakespeare, *yet* he enjoyed the play.

A compound sentence can also be two simple sentences joined by a semicolon.

> He didn't think he was a fan of Shakespeare; he enjoyed the play.

Match It

Match simple sentences in Column A with simple sentences in Column B to create compound sentences. Write the compound sentences and remember to add either a coordinate conjunction or punctuation.

Column A

1. The football game was exciting.

2. My favorite team is playing.

3. My school's colors are blue and white.

4. I'm going to get a pretzel at halftime.

5. My team won the game.

Column B

1. They have a good record this year.

2. I'm going to get pizza after the game.

3. The score was close.

4. The season isn't over yet.

5. The opposing team's colors are green and gold.

1. _____

_____

2. _____

_____

3. _____

_____

4. _____

_____

5. _____

_____

Lesson 1.28 Compound Sentences

Rewrite It
Rewrite the following paragraph, changing simple sentences to compound sentences. Combine the sentences with coordinate conjunctions or semicolons.

What Is a triathlon?

A triathlon is a unique sporting event. Three different sports are involved. Participants in a triathlon swim, bike, and run. It is a challenging event. The very first triathlon was held in France in 1921. The name of the event was Course Des Trois Sports (The Race of Three Sports). The first American triathlon was in 1974. It took place in San Diego, California. Hundreds of athletes now participate in triathlons. There's a distance for everyone. The shortest distance is the sprint distance. It consists of a 400-1000 yard swim, an 8-20 mile bike ride, and a 2-5 mile run. The international distance is also the Olympic distance. It has a 1 mile swim, a 24.8 mile bike ride, and a 6.2 mile run. The Ironman is the king of triathlons. It consists of a 2.4 mile swim, a 112 mile bike ride, and a 26.2 mile run. Triathlons are quite challenging. It is not enough. Of course we are always pushing ourselves harder and harder. Now athletes take part in ultratriathlons. What will be next?

_____
_____
_____
_____
_____
_____
_____
_____
_____
_____
_____
_____
_____
_____
_____
_____
_____
_____

Lesson 1.29 Complex Sentences

Complex sentences have one independent clause and one or more dependent clauses. The independent and dependent clauses are connected with a subordinate conjunction or a relative pronoun. Dependent clauses do not present a complete thought and cannot stand alone as sentences. The dependent clause can be anywhere in the sentence.

Complex sentence (connected with subordinate conjunction):
> You can go to the movies *if* you finish your homework.

Complex sentence (connected with a relative pronoun):
> My mother asked me to drop off these flowers for Mrs. Hastings, *whose* house is on our way to school.

Dependent clauses follow the connecting subordinate conjunction or the relative pronoun. The dependent clause can either be the first or second part of the sentence.
> *Before* the movie, I'll finish my homework.
> I'll finish my homework *before* the movie.

Identify It
Put a checkmark on the line following the complex sentences.

1. _____ I like biking because it is good exercise.

2. _____ Tony is going to order pasta with mushrooms, which is his favorite dish.

3. _____ History is my favorite subject.

4. _____ Mr. Baum, who is also the baseball coach, is my favorite teacher.

5. _____ While Kim is a good speller, Jerry is better.

6. _____ I would like a salad for lunch, yet soup sounds good, too.

7. _____ Erin made the basketball team after two weeks of tryouts.

8. _____ Although it's going to snow, I think we should still hike the trails.

9. _____ Unless it rains, we'll walk, not ride.

10. _____ We can continue hiking until it gets icy.

Lesson 1.29 Complex Sentences

Solve It

Find the subordinate conjunctions from the box in the puzzle. Words can be horizontal, vertical, forward, backward, or diagonal.

after	before	that	when
although	if	though	where
as	since	unless	whereas
because	so	until	while

```
b  c  i  a  a  e  l  i  h  w
e  e  f  s  h  s  t  n  t  h
f  s  c  c  w  h  e  n  j  e
o  r  m  a  c  e  l  e  b  r
r  i  i  t  u  n  t  i  l  e
e  e  c  n  i  s  t  e  v  a
y  c  h  e  f  h  e  a  e  s
s  o  n  t  g  r  m  a  h  r
a  t  h  u  n  l  e  s  s  t
o  n  o  a  z  b  y  t  c  x
w  h  e  r  e  d  v  e  f  u
t  f  h  g  u  o  h  t  l  a
```

Try It

Write three complex sentences (one of each type from page 64). Write about your favorite sporting event or your favorite subject at school.

1. _____

   _____

2. _____

   _____

3. _____

   _____

Lesson 1.30 Sentence Fragments

A **sentence fragment** is a group of words that is missing a subject, predicate, or both. A sentence fragment is also a group of words that doesn't express a complete thought, as in a dependent clause.

Doesn't have good insulation. (no subject)
Complete Sentence: The window doesn't have good insulation.

The window good insulation. (no predicate)
Complete Sentence: The window doesn't have good insulation.

Good insulation. (no subject or predicate)
Complete Sentence: The window doesn't have good insulation.

Since the lemonade was too sour. (not a complete thought)
Complete Sentence: We drank water since the lemonade was too sour.

Complete It

Complete the following sentence fragments by choosing a sentence fragment from the box that completes the sentences.

> **It was presented** **Construction began**
> **The statue's height** **is "Liberty Enlightening the World."**
> **stands on Liberty Island in the New York Harbor.**

1. The Statue of Liberty _____
_____. (look for a verb phrase)

2. _____ in France in 1875.
(look for a subject and a verb)

3. _____ to the United
States on July 4, 1884. (look for a subject and verb)

4. The official name of the Statue of Liberty _____
_____. (look for a verb phrase)

5. _____
from base to torch is 152 feet, 2 inches. (look for a subject)

Lesson 1.30 Sentence Fragments

Identify It
Identify the following sentences as either sentence fragments or complete sentences. Write an **F** for *fragment* and a **CS** for *complete sentence*. Then, for the sentences that are fragments, tell why they are fragments (e.g. missing a subject). Write your answer on the line below each sentence.

1. The satellite is orbiting Mars.

_____ _____

2. As though the sun were shining.

_____ _____

3. is my favorite song.

_____ _____

4. in the morning.

_____ _____

5. in the evening.

_____ _____

6. My best friend is my dog Spike.

_____ _____

7. Since the whole class is going on the field trip.

_____ _____

8. is my favorite subject in school.

_____ _____

Try It
Several of the sentences above are fragments. Complete 6 of these sentences by adding subjects and/or predicates of your own.

1. _____
2. _____
3. _____
4. _____
5. _____
6. _____

Lesson 1.31 Combining Sentences

Combining short, choppy sentences into longer more detailed sentences makes writing much more interesting and easier to read. Sentences can be combined in a variety of ways.

Compound Subjects and Compound Verbs:

The lightning is coming. The thunder is coming.
The *thunder and lightning* are coming.

The president of our class is honest. The president of our class is loyal.
The president of our class is *honest and loyal*.

Adjectives and Adverbs:

I went to a party. The party was a costume party.
I went to a *costume party*.

Timothy ran quickly. Timothy ran in the race.
Timothy *ran quickly* in the race.

Making Complex Sentences (using subordinate conjunctions):

Donna wanted to go to the reunion. Donna wanted to go *if* her best friend Diane went.
Donna wanted to go to the reunion, if her best friend Diane went.

Match It

Under Column A are five combined sentences. Under Column B are the parts of speech that were combined. Match the sentences in Column A with the parts of speech in Column B.

Column A

1. The salesman reluctantly attended the seminar.

2. Dan and Rose are taking swimming lessons.

3. Cam's parents lived in a beautiful neighborhood.

4. David climbed and descended the mountain.

5. The phone rang while we were eating.

Column B

combined subjects

combined verbs

combined adjective

combined adverb

subordinate conjunction

Lesson 1.31 Combining Sentences

Rewrite It

Rewrite the following paragraphs by combining simple sentences into compound or complex sentences.

Charles Schulz was one of America's most famous cartoonists. He created the most popular comic strip ever. He wrote the most popular comic strip ever: *Peanuts*. The *Peanuts* characters are some of the most popular characters ever seen in comic strips, in books, and on television. The *Peanuts* comic strip made its debut in seven newspapers in 1950.

Schulz actually had a black and white dog named Spike. Spike was the inspiration for Snoopy. Snoopy is the world's most famous beagle. Schulz based much of *Peanuts* on his own life. The *Peanuts* characters teach us all lessons about ourselves. They teach us about the the world around us.

_____

_____

_____

_____

_____

_____

_____

_____

_____

_____

_____

_____

Try It

Write five combined sentences of your own. Write one sentence with compound subjects, one with compound verbs, one with combined adjectives, one with combined adverbs, and one using a subordinate conjunction.

1. _____

2. _____

3. _____

4. _____

5. _____

Lesson 1.32 Writing a Paragraph

A **paragraph** is made up of a group of sentences. A paragraph should have, and stick to, a single topic. Each sentence of the paragraph should focus on the topic with plenty of information and supporting details related to the topic.

Elements of a Paragraph: There are three parts to a paragraph.

1. Beginning: The topic sentence is the beginning of the paragraph. It tells the reader what the paragraph is going to be about. It expresses the feeling of the paragraph.

2. Middle: The middle is the main element of the paragraph. The sentences here give more information and supporting details about the topic sentence.

3. End: After all of the information and details are written, the end sentence sums it all up.

Writing the Paragraph: There are five steps to take when writing a paragraph.

1. Prewriting: Choose your topic and think about what information you want to include.

2. Drafting: Write your topic sentence and the other parts of your paragraph.

3. Revising: Reread your paragraph. Make sure the three parts of your paragraph are used correctly. Rewrite your paragraph and include details with adjectives and adverbs to make it more interesting.

4. Proofreading: Proofread your paragraph looking for errors in spelling and punctuation.

5. Publishing: Now's your chance to show off your work. You will publish your paragraph.

Types of Paragraphs: A few of the most common paragraphs include the following types:

Descriptive – Descriptive paragraphs give vivid details of people, places, things, or ideas.

Narrative – Narrative paragraphs give the details of an event or events in the form of a story.

Expository – Expository paragraphs give facts or explain ideas in a nonfiction format.

Persuasive – Persuasive paragraphs express an opinion and try to convince readers that this opinion is correct.

Lesson 1.32 Writing a Paragraph

Rewrite It

The sentences in the following paragraph are out of order. Rewrite the paragraph placing the topic sentence first, the summary sentence last, and the body sentences in between.

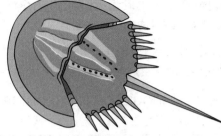

This substance has a red pigment. Horseshoe crabs' blood has copper in it. Not all living creatures have red blood; horseshoe crabs' blood is blue! Human blood has hemoglobin that has iron in it. The color of one's blood, whether a creature big or small, depends on the makeup and chemicals in the blood. This material causes the blood to appear blue.

topic sentence: _____

_____

first body sentence: _____

_____

second body sentence: _____

_____

third body sentence: _____

_____

fourth body sentence: _____

_____

end sentence: _____

_____

Try It

Write a paragraph about a topic of your choosing. Select one of the types of paragraphs. Think about your topic ideas and the five steps of writing.

_____

_____

_____

_____

_____

_____

_____

Review Chapter 1 Lessons 26–32

Review: Declarative Sentences, Interrogative Sentences, Exclamatory Sentences, Imperative Sentences

Putting It Together

Rewrite the exclamatory sentence as an imperative sentence.

1. You should drink the hot tea slowly!

_____

Rewrite the interrogative sentence as a declarative sentence.

2. Are you going to the game on Saturday?

_____

Rewrite the imperative sentence as an interrogative sentence.

3. Hit the ball far!

_____

Rewrite the declarative sentence as an imperative sentence.

4. You should recycle the papers instead of putting them in the trash.

_____

Review: Simple Sentences, Compound Sentences, Complex Sentences, Sentence Fragments, Combining Sentences

Write whether the following sentences are simple, compound, complex, or a sentence fragment. If they are simple sentences or sentence fragments, rewrite them.

1. She jogged through the mist. She jogged slowly.

_____

2. The chefs cooked and baked in the competition.

_____

3. After dinner, I'm going for a walk.

_____

4. Although I studied hard,

_____

Review Chapter 1 Lessons 26–32

Review: Writing a Paragraph

1. What is one of the most important things to do when writing a paragraph?

   _____

2. If you were asked to write a paragraph about your favorite animal, what type of paragraph would that be?

   _____

3. What do you write in the last sentence of a paragraph?

   _____

4. If you were asked to write a paragraph that tries to convince your readers of something, what type of paragraph would that be?

   _____

5. What is the body of a paragraph?

   _____

Now, write a short paragraph about your favorite movie. Remember to use the different parts of a paragraph.

_____

_____

_____

_____

_____

_____

_____

_____

_____

_____

_____

_____

_____

Lesson 2.1 Proper Nouns: Days of the Week, Months of the Year

Proper nouns are specific people, places, and things. They are capitalized.

Capitalize days of the week.

Sunday Monday Tuesday Wednesday Thursday Friday Saturday

Capitalize months of the year.

January February March April May June July August September
October November December

Months of the year are also capitalized when they serve as adjectives.

They ran the marathon on a sunny *June* morning.

Solve It

Complete the following sentences by cracking the code and filling in the blanks. Remember to capitalize the days of the weeks when you write them.

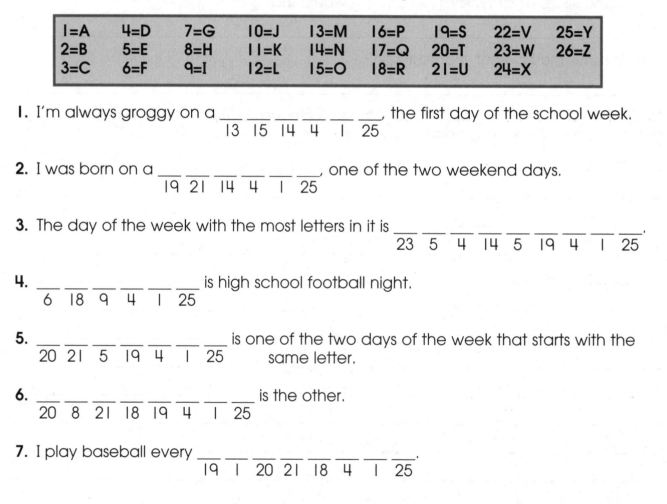

1=A	4=D	7=G	10=J	13=M	16=P	19=S	22=V	25=Y
2=B	5=E	8=H	11=K	14=N	17=Q	20=T	23=W	26=Z
3=C	6=F	9=I	12=L	15=O	18=R	21=U	24=X	

1. I'm always groggy on a ___ ___ ___ ___ ___ ___, the first day of the school week.
   13 15 14 4 1 25

2. I was born on a ___ ___ ___ ___ ___ ___, one of the two weekend days.
   19 21 14 4 1 25

3. The day of the week with the most letters in it is ___ ___ ___ ___ ___ ___ ___ ___ ___.
   23 5 4 14 5 19 4 1 25

4. ___ ___ ___ ___ ___ ___ is high school football night.
   6 18 9 4 1 25

5. ___ ___ ___ ___ ___ ___ ___ is one of the two days of the week that starts with the same letter.
   20 21 5 19 4 1 25

6. ___ ___ ___ ___ ___ ___ ___ ___ is the other.
   20 8 21 18 19 4 1 25

7. I play baseball every ___ ___ ___ ___ ___ ___ ___ ___.
   19 1 20 21 18 4 1 25

Lesson 2.1 Proper Nouns: Days of the Week, Months of the Year

Rewrite It
Rewrite the following sentences after unscrambling the names of the months. Do not forget to capitalize them.

1. The month of <u>jeun</u> is Adopt a Shelter Cat Month.

   _____

2. Earth Day, a day for environmental awareness, is celebrated in <u>lpari</u>.

   _____

3. Adopt a Shelter Dog Month is held in <u>cbotore</u>.

   _____

4. St. Valentine is credited for bringing couples together on the 14th of <u>barufrey</u>.

   _____

5. The state of Colorado has its own day, and it's celebrated in <u>stuagu</u>.

   _____

6. Shogatsu is the name for New Year in Japan; it is celebrated in <u>najruay</u>.

   _____

Try It
Write a paragraph about your favorite day of the week or month of the year.

_____
_____
_____
_____
_____
_____
_____
_____
_____
_____
_____

Lesson 2.2 Proper Nouns: Historical Events, Names of Languages and Nationalities, Team Names

Historical events, nationalities, and team names are **proper nouns**, as well.

Events, periods of time, and important documents from history are capitalized.
Cold War   Renaissance Period   Constitution of the United States

Names of languages and nationalities are capitalized. They are also capitalized when they are used as adjectives.
French   Hispanic   Dutch apple pie

The names of sports teams are capitalized.
Detroit Tigers

Complete It
Complete the following sentences by circling the correct answer in parentheses. Hint: not all choices are proper and need to be capitalized.

1. The war lasting from 1939 to 1945 was (world war II, World War II).

2. The (italian, Italian) language is one of the romance languages.

3. An (era, Era) is considered to be any important period of time.

4. The season begins for (baseball teams, Baseball Teams) in April.

5. Mikhail Baryshnikov is of (russian, Russian) descent.

6. The (boston red sox, Boston Red Sox) won the World Series in 2004.

7. The (*magna carta, Magna Carta*) was written in 1215.

8. The (english, English) cocker spaniel was the number one dog in popularity in Britain from the 1930s through the 1950s.

9. The (victorian era, Victorian Era) lasted from 1839 to 1901, during the reign of Queen Victoria in England.

10. The (french, French) soufflé is a dessert served warm.

11. The first ten amendments to the *Constitution of the United States* is the (bill of rights, Bill of Rights).

12. The (battle of waterloo, Battle of Waterloo) took place in Belgium in 1815.

Lesson 2.2 Proper Nouns: Historical Events, Names of Languages and Nationalities, Team Names

Solve It
Unscramble the following letters in parentheses to complete each sentence with a word from the box. Capitalize each word when necessary.

period address	patriots angels	world german	war greek

1. The Jurassic _____ (rdieop) was a period in time that saw the rise of the dinosaurs.

2. _____ (rowdl) War II ended in Japan on V-J Day on September 2, 1945.

3. A famous speech was the Gettysburg _____ (dresads) given by Abraham Lincoln.

4. The _____ (mgnare) chocolate cake did not really originate in Germany.

5. The New England _____ (strapiot) football team has a patriotic mascot.

6. World _____ (rwa) I was also known as the *Great War*.

7. An angelic baseball team might be known as the Los Angeles _____ (saenlg).

8. The Greeks were the first Europeans to use an alphabet, what became known as the _____ (ekreg) alphabet.

Try It
Write a paragraph about your favorite sports team. Don't forget to use capitals when needed.

_____

_____

_____

_____

_____

_____

_____

_____

Lesson 2.3 Proper Nouns: Organizations, Departments of Government, Sections of the Country

Organizations, departments of government, and sections of the country are all **proper nouns** and are capitalized.

The names of organizations and associations are capitalized.

Capital Area Humane Society   Microsoft Corporation

Capitalize the names of departments of government.

Department of Treasury   Department of Health and Human Services

Directional words that point out particular sections of the country are capitalized. However, words that give directions are not capitalized.

Heather grew up on the *East Coast* of the United States.
Madilyn grew up on the *east side* of town.

Identify It

Circle the name of the organization, department of government, or section of the country in each sentence.

1. My mom and dad work for the Department of Transportation.

2. Tina and her family are moving to the Midwest this summer.

3. The National Aeronautics and Space Administration is in charge of space exploration.

4. I volunteer for the American Red Cross.

5. San Francisco is on the West Coast of the United States.

6. While walking to school, we pass the Smithson Art Association.

7. We are traveling to the Southwest next year.

8. Tasha's aunt works for the State Department.

9. Have you ever been to New England?

10. We must send in our tax forms by April 15 to the Internal Revenue Service.

11. TransUnion Carrier Services provides cardboard boxes for moving.

12. Portland, Oregon is in the Northwest.

Lesson 2.3 Proper Nouns: Organizations, Departments of Government, Sections of the Country

Proof It
Proofread the following sentences. Some of the words should be capitalized and are not. Some are capitalized that should not be.

> ≡ – capitalize letter
> / – lowercase letter

1. A nonprofit organization with human service programs is the volunteers of America.

2. The National Parks Service is a part of the department of the interior.

3. The northwest can be a rainy part of the country.

4. The mountains of Virginia are in the Western part of the state.

5. The sheraton corporation is a hospitality network.

6. The Administration for Children and Families is a part of the department of health and human services.

7. Summer occurs in the southern Hemisphere between December and February.

8. The Atlantic Ocean lies in the Eastern part of the United States.

9. A good collection of young adult literature can be found at baldwin public library.

10. Black beans and spices are often found in southwestern cooking.

Try It
Scan a local newspaper looking for organizations and departments of government that use capital letters. Write down all that you find.

_____

_____

_____

_____

_____

_____

_____

_____

Lesson 2.4 Proper Nouns: Titles, Geographic Names

The titles of books, poems, songs, movies, plays, newspapers, and magazines are **proper nouns** and are capitalized. Most titles are also underlined in text. Song titles and essays, however, are in quotes.

> book: _The Cat in the Hat_   song: "Atomic Dog"   magazine: _Time_

Titles associated with names are also capitalized.

> _Mayor_ Franklin   _Senator_ Santos   _Professor_ Johnson

Do not capitalize these titles if they are not directly used with the name.

> The _mayor_ of our town is _Mayor_ Franklin.

Geographic names, such as the names of countries, states, cities, counties, bodies of water, public areas, roads and highways, and buildings are capitalized.

> _Columbia, Hawaii, Athens, Chesapeake Bay, Sierra Nevada Range, Rocky Mountain National Park, Paint Creek Trail, Globe Theatre_

If the geographic name is not a specific name, do not capitalize it.

> I'm going to _the lake_ for the weekend.

Complete It

Complete the following sentences by circling the best answer in parentheses.

1. My favorite song is ("Vertigo", "vertigo") by U2.

2. The (President, president) of the organization is visiting on Tuesday.

3. At 2:00 pm, (Governor, governor) Spencer is making a speech.

4. Valerie and Gerald watched the sunset from the (Eiffel Tower, eiffel tower).

5. Are you going to the (Mountains, mountains) or the beach for vacation?

6. One of my favorite books is (<u>The Elephant Hospital</u>, <u>the elephant hospital</u>).

7. Lynda walks in a park along the (Scioto River, scioto river).

8. The (Martin Luther King, Jr. Highway, Martin Luther King, Jr. highway) is located in Washington, D.C.

9. My cousin was born in (Birmingham, birmingham), England.

10. The tiny (Village, village) sits next to a canal.

Lesson 2.4 Proper Nouns: Titles, Geographic Names

Find It
Answer the following questions. If you need help, use an
encyclopedia or other resource. Be sure to capitalize the answers
when necessary.

1. Who is the principal of your school? _____

2. What city, state, and country do you live in? _____

3. Where were you born? _____

4. Who is the governor of your state? _____

5. What is your favorite book? _____

6. What is your favorite movie? _____

7. What is your favorite poem? _____

8. What states border the state in which you live? _____

9. What is the closest national park to where you live? _____

10. What is the name of your local newspaper? _____

11. What magazine do you like to read the most? _____

12. What is the name of one of your state's senators? _____

Try It
Use the information gathered above to write a brief biography about yourself. As in
your previous answers, remember to capitalize titles and geographic names when
necessary. You can also include other information about yourself in addition to the
facts above.

_____

_____

_____

_____

_____

_____

_____

_____

_____

_____

Lesson 2.5 Sentences, Direct Quotations

The first word of every **sentence** is capitalized.
> *The* wind blew strongly through the trees.

The first word in **direct quotations** is also capitalized.
> My father said, "*Finish* your homework and then we'll go for a ride."
> "*I'm* almost finished now," I happily answered.

Indirect quotations are not capitalized.
> My father said he had been working on his car for weeks.

If a continuous sentence in a direct quotation is split and the second half is not a new sentence, do not capitalize it. If a new sentence begins after the split, then capitalize it as you would with any sentence.
> "Keep your hands and arms inside the car," said the attendant, "*and* stay seated."
> "Roller coasters are my favorite rides," I said. "*I* can ride them all day."

Complete It
Complete the following sentences by circling the best answer in parentheses.

1. (The, the) girls' team beat the boys' team by three seconds.

2. T.C. said, "(Baseball, baseball) is my favorite sport."

3. "(Put, put) your donated clothing in plastic bags," said the event organizer.

4. The technician said (The, the) car would be ready in a few hours.

5. "Don't rush through your homework," said the teacher, "(And, and) stay focused."

6. "Be careful as you shovel the snow," mother said. "(You, you) can hurt your back."

7. (The, the) airplane was going to be delayed.

8. Renee said, "(Would, would) you like a baseball hat when we go to the park?"

9. "(Our, our) race will begin in 10 minutes," said the announcer.

10. The sales clerk said (She, she) would hold the item for one day.

11. "Lemon cream is my favorite pie," said Lisa, "(But, but) nothing beats brownies."

12. "I can't wait until my birthday," said Jack. "(My, my) parents are giving me a party."

Lesson 2.5 Sentences, Direct Quotations

Proof It
Proofread the following dialogue
correcting capitalization errors.

^	– inserts correct words or punctuation
≡	– capitalize letter

"Hi, Dad," said Jack. "we learned about tsunamis today."

"what did you learn about tsunamis?" Jack's dad asked.

Jack answered, "well, we learned that tsunamis can move up to 500 miles per

hour. we also learned about how they are formed."

"the earth's crust is made up of interlocking plates," said Jack. "the plates are

floating on a hot, flexible interior that drifts. The plates sometimes collide. In a

subduction, an ocean plate slides under continental plates. Over the years, the plates

lock, the seafloor compresses, and the coastline warps up. eventually, the pressure

pops and the seafloor lunges landward. The coast lunges seaward. the plates push

seawater all over, creating the tsunami. Geologists can study sedimentary layers near

the seaside to tell when shifts have occurred in the past, maybe helping to understand

when it might happen again."

Try It
Write a dialogue between you and a friend, teacher, or parent. Explain to the other
person something you learned about in school. Remember the capitalization rules.

_____

_____

_____

_____

_____

_____

_____

_____

_____

_____

Lesson 2.6 Personal and Business Letters

A **personal letter** has five parts: heading, salutation, body, closing, and signature.

The **heading** of a personal letter is the address of the person writing the letter and the date it is written. The name of the street, the city, the state, and the month are all capitalized.

> 1245 Hollow Dr.
> Suncrest, AZ
> March 31, 2008

The **salutation** is the greeting and begins with the word *dear*. Both *dear* and the name of the person who is receiving the letter are capitalized. The salutation ends with a comma.

> Dear Stanley,

The **body** is the main part of the letter and contains sentences that are capitalized as normal.

The **closing** can be written in many ways; only the first word is capitalized.

> Your friend,   Sincerely,   All the best,

The **signature** is usually only your first name in a personal letter. It is also always capitalized.

> Milton

Identify It

Identify the parts of the personal letter by writing the names on the lines provided. Then, circle the capital letters.

7511 Hibernia Rd.

_____ Seattle, WA 40000

February 31, 2008

Dear Uncle Josh, _____

    How are you? My ski trip has been great. I even learned how to snowboard. I think I'll be really sore tomorrow. All of the fundraising was worth it. Thanks for helping us out. I'm glad our class got to take this trip. I hope I'll get to come back someday. _____

        Thank you, _____

        Mike _____

Lesson 2.6 Personal and Business Letters

A **business letter** has six parts: heading, inside address, salutation, body, closing and signature.

The **heading** of a business letter is the address of the person writing the letter and the date it is written. The name of the street, the city, the state, and the month are all capitalized.

> 4003 Fourteenth St.
> Amlin, NH 20000
> September 6, 2008

The **inside address** includes the name and complete address of the person to whom the letter is going.

> Mark Dillon, Director
> S.A.S Productions
> 100 Otterbein Ave.
> Rochester, NY 20000

The **salutation** is the greeting and begins with the word *dear*. Both *dear* and the name of the person who is receiving the letter are capitalized. The salutation ends with a colon.

> Dear Director:

The **body** is the main part of the letter and contains sentences that are capitalized as normal.

The **closing** can be written many ways. Only the first word is capitalized.

> Yours truly,   Sincerely,   Very truly,

The **signature** is your full name and is capitalized.

> Leigh D. McGregor

Try It
Write the heading, inside address, salutation, closing, and signature of a business letter. Make up the names and other information, but be sure you capitalize correctly.

heading: _____   inside address: _____

        _____   _____

        _____   _____

salutation: _____   closing: _____

signature: _____

Review Chapter 2 Lessons 2.1–2.6

Review: Capitalization: Proper Nouns: Days of the Week; Months of the Year; Historical Events; Names of Languages and Nationalities; Team Names; Organizations; Departments of Government; Sections of the Country; Sentences; Direct Quotations

Putting It Together

Complete the following sentences by circling the best answer in parentheses.

1. "Riley," called Gillian, "(Let's, let's) use carrots and raisins on our snowman."

2. Our teacher said the test will be on (Wednesday, wednesday).

3. (Winters, winters) in the north are cold and blustery.

4. The summer solstice occurs in the month of (June, june).

5. Drive (North, north) on Route 3 and then you'll be close to the community center.

6. The hostess said, "(Your, your) table will be ready in 10 minutes."

7. The U.S. (Constitution, constitution) was drawn in Philadelphia in 1787.

8. The (Peace Corp, peace corp) is a federal agency that reports to Congress and the Executive Branch.

9. "(My, my) shift starts at 3:00, so let's study when I'm finished." said Celia.

10. The high school offers (Italian, italian) as one of its languages.

11. The (Aveda Corporation, aveda corporation) is located in Minnesota.

12. North America is located in the (Northern, northern) hemisphere.

13. In the fairy tale, the princess said (She, she) was waiting for her prince.

14. The (Danish, danish) pastry is baked fresh every day.

15. My favorite baseball team is the (San Francisco Giants, San Francisco giants).

16. The pep rally will be held in the gym on (Friday, friday) afternoon.

17. The (Sierra Club, sierra club) is an environmental organization for people of all ages.

18. Doug said, "(My, my) Aunt Clara makes the best blueberry muffins."

19. Samuel Adams and Paul Revere were two of the colonists who initiated the events of the (Boston Tea Party, Boston tea party).

20. The winter solstice occurs in the month of (December, december).

21. The bus driver said (Traffic, traffic) was causing delays.

22. Surfing is popular on the (North, north) Coast of Oahu.

Review Chapter 2 Lessons 2.1–2.6

Review: Capitalization: Personal Letters, Business Letters

Putting It Together
Proofread the following business letter. Make all necessary capitalization corrections.

≡ – capitalize letter

105 front street
Norfolk, VA 20000
april 17, 2008

Mr. Henry Munson, director
Student Volunteer Programs
242 W. 29th street
New York, NY 30000

dear Mr. Munson:

My name is John Burg and I am a seventh-grader at Houghton junior high school in Norfolk, Virginia. I would like to apply for a position with the Student Volunteer Save the Turtle Program.

I am on the basketball and track teams. I also write for our school paper. I am also a junior member of our local chapter of the sierra club. I have researched the Save the Turtle Program and would be honored to be a member of the upcoming team.

included with this letter are my application and a list of references. I look forward to having a phone interview with you to further discuss your programs. thank you for your time.

sincerely,

John Burg

John Burg

Lesson 2.7 Periods: After Imperative Sentences, In Dialogue, In Abbreviations, In Initials

Sometimes, imperative sentences call for a **period**, as when the sentence is not urgent.
Pay the toll at the booth.

Periods are used in dialogue. The period goes inside the quotation mark.
Jean said, "Give Mimi a drink of water."

If the quote comes at the beginning of the sentence, use a comma at the end of the direct quotation and before the quotation mark. Place a period at the end of the sentence.
"If it gets cold, put on your jacket," said Robyn.

Use a period after each part of an abbreviation. Use a period after each letter of an initial.
M.A. (Master of Arts)   Samuel L. Jackson

Complete It

Complete the following sentences by adding periods where necessary.

1. Check out at the far counter

   _____

2. Janet said, "Let's take a long walk"

   _____

3. "Hiking is my favorite hobby," said Charlie

   _____

4. Kathryn received her MA from the University of Arizona.

   _____

5. My favorite actress is Vivica A Fox.

   _____

6. "Jump over the puddle, so you will stay dry," yelled Eddie

   _____

7. Reach a little farther, and you will have touched the top

   _____

8. JRR Tolkein is my favorite author.

   _____

Lesson 2.7 # Periods: After Imperative Sentences, In Dialogue, In Abbreviations, In Initials

Proof It

Proofread the following recipe. Add periods after imperative sentences and in abbreviations where they are necessary.

⊙ – inserts period

Homemade Hummus

4 cups cooked & drained garbanzo beans

1 cup tahini

1 cup fresh lemon juice

6 tbs (tablespoons) olive oil

$\frac{3}{4}$ cup minced garlic

1 tsp (teaspoon) salt

1 tsp (teaspoon) black pepper

Place all ingredients in a large mixing bowl Mash ingredients with a fork and then blend well Store hummus covered in the refrigerator Remove hummus from refrigerator when ready to serve Sprinkle hummus with paprika Serve hummus at room temperature Recipe serves 12-15

Try It

Write your favorite recipe. Don't forget the periods after abbreviations.

_____

_____

_____

_____

_____

_____

_____

_____

_____

Lesson 2.9 Question Marks

Question marks are used in sentences that ask questions, called interrogative sentences.

> How was your trip**?**

When used in quotations, questions marks can be placed either inside or outside of the end quotation mark depending on the meaning of the sentence.

When the question mark is punctuating the quotation itself, it is placed inside the quote.

> The coach asked, "How many push-ups can you do**?**"

When the question mark is punctuating the entire sentence, it is placed outside the quote.

> Did the coach say, "Try to do twice as many as you did last week"**?**

A question mark is not used in sentences with indirect quotations.

> Suhad asked the librarian for help finding the book**.**

Match It

Draw a line to match the sentences in Column A with their descriptions in Column B.

Column A

1. Bill asked the guide how long the museum would be open.

2. Could you tell that funny joke again?

3. Sylvia's mother asked, "What time is your track meet on Saturday?"

4. Did the weather reporter say, "Expect six inches of snow tonight"?

Column B

interrogative sentence

question mark punctuating quotation

question mark punctuating entire sentence

indirect quotation

---

5. Where did you park the car?

6. Did you say, "Read page four"?

7. Sam asked for a quarter to make a wish in the well.

8. The teacher asked, "What is the square root of 64?"

interrogative sentence

question mark punctuating quotation

question mark punctuating entire sentence

indirect quotation

Lesson 2.9 Question Marks

Proof It
Proofread the following dialogue correcting the misplaced and misused question marks.

| " " / ∨ | – inserts quotations |
| ↶ | – moves letters, words, punctuation, text from one location to another |

"Dr. Edwards," asked Eric, "what should I study in school if I want to be a vet"?

Dr. Edwards answered, Eric, anyone who wants to be a vet should study math and science. Veterinarians have to go to medical school, just like people doctors. They have to know how much and which medicines to prescribe." Dr. Edwards continued, "You must also be good at social skills."

"I like working with people. Is that important"? asked Eric.

Oh, yes," exclaimed Dr. Edwards. "Doctors have to listen to their patients. In this case, the patients' guardians have to speak for them. I listen very carefully to help with my diagnosis. Sometimes, vets have to discuss serious matters with the guardians."

Eric asked the doctor what was the most important quality for a vet to possess.

"Veterinarians must love animals," answered Dr. Edwards. "We care for them and their guardians in the very best way we can. Do you still want to be a vet, Eric"?

"Absolutely! answered Eric.

Try It
Write three sentences using question marks: one interrogative sentence, one sentence where the question mark punctuates the quotation, and one sentence where the question mark punctuates the entire sentence.

_____

_____

_____

_____

Lesson 2.10 Exclamation Points

Exclamation points are used at the end of sentences that express surprise and strong emotion, called exclamatory sentences.

We have to read all three chapters for homework!

Interjections sometimes require exclamation points.

Ah ha! I've come up with the answer!

If you use an exclamation point, make sure the sentence expresses surprise, urgency, or strong emotion. Don't overuse exclamation points.

Complete It

Complete the following sentences by circling the best end punctuation in parentheses.

1. Can bees talk (. ?)

2. Scientists have discovered that bees do communicate with each other (. !)

3. How do they talk (? !)

4. Bees don't talk with their voices (. !)

5. Bees talk through dance (? !)

6. What do bees talk about (. ?)

7. Bees talk about gathering food (. !)

8. One dance move tells where the food is located (. ?)

9. Another dance move tells how far the food is away (. !)

10. Are there more dance moves (? !)

11. Yes, another move tells about how much food is in a particular location (. ?)

12. Do dancing bees have a special name (? !)

13. The bees who communicate about the food are called scout bees (. !)

14. Scout bees dance for forager bees (. ?)

15. Forager bees interpret the dance and go out to get the food (. ?)

16. How do the forager bees understand what the moves mean (? !)

17. How fast the scouts dance tells how far the food is away (. ?)

18. The angle the scouts dance tells where the food is and the number of times the scouts dance tells how much food there is (. ?)

19. What an amazing story (? !)

20. Bees are amazing creatures (. !)

Lesson 2.10 Exclamation Points

Solve It
Choose a word from the box to complete the following sentences so they express strong emotion or surprise. Not all words will be used.

brave	fast	loud	show	tall
cautious	freezing	low	short	tied
close	high	luke warm	soft	warm
far	hot	mild	spicy	won

1. Don't touch the stove, it is _____!

2. Look how _____ that racecar driver took the curve!

3. Please turn down that _____ music!

4. The trapeze performer is so _____ from the ground!

5. This tour through the caves is scary; the walls are too _____!

6. It's cold outside and the water is _____!

7. The astronauts on this mission are so _____!

8. Be careful when you take a bite, the dip is very _____!

9. Yea! Our team _____ the championship!

10. The sequoia tree is so _____!

Try It
Write a paragraph describing an exciting sporting event in which you participated or watched. Use exclamation points where appropriate.

_____

_____

_____

_____

_____

_____

_____

Lesson 2.11 Commas: Series, Direct Address, Multiple Adjectives

Commas have a variety of uses, such as in a series, in direct address, and with multiple adjectives.

Series commas are used when there is at least three items listed in a sentence in a row. The items can be words or phrases. Commas are used to separate them.

My favorite foods are *pizza, pasta salad, and vegetable burritos.*
To make a pizza you have to *roll the crust, spread the sauce, and add the toppings.*

Commas are used to separate the name of a person spoken to from the rest of the sentence. This is called a **direct address**.

Ken, please answer the door.   Your delivery has arrived, *Adam.*

When more than one adjective is used to describe a noun, they are separated by commas.

It was a *warm, breezy* day.

Make sure the adjectives equally modify the noun, and that one item is not actually an adverb modifying the adjective. There is no comma in the following sentence because *hilariously* is an adverb modifying *funny,* not *book.*

Calvin read a *hilariously funny book.*

Identify It
Write an **S** for series, a **DA** for direct address, or an **MA** for multiple adjectives.

1. _____ Before you leave for school, eat your breakfast, put your homework in your backpack, and brush your teeth.

2. _____ I had a sweet, juicy apple for lunch.

3. _____ Finish your homework before playing video games, Craig.

4. _____ Shawn had a long, hard homework assignment.

5. _____ Chloe, your song in the concert was beautiful.

6. _____ Don't forget your maps, food, and water for your hiking trip.

7. _____ Trevor, wash your hands before dinner.

8. _____ I grabbed a book, paper, and a pencil from my desk when packing for our trip.

9. _____ It was a cold, blustery day.

Lesson 2.11 Commas: Series, Direct Address, Multiple Adjectives

Proof It
Rewrite the following dialogue, adding commas where they are needed.

˄, – inserts a comma

"Reese guess what I'm doing this weekend," said Dani.

"Are you going to play basketball at the school clean your room at home or finish your science report?" answered Reese.

"None of the above, Reese" Dani said grinning. "I'm going to the best brightest show on the planet. My grandparents are taking me to see Cirque du Soleil."

Reese replied, "Isn't that the circus with only human performers?"

"Yep, that's the one," answered Dani. "The brave talented acrobats do all kinds of maneuvers high in the air on ropes. They dance swing and fly through the air."

"I think I even heard that they do some acts underwater!" said Reese.

"They also have hysterically funny clowns," added Dani. "I've heard that sometimes they even spray water on the audience!"

"I've got a nice big surprise for you Reese," beamed Dani. "My grandparents got tickets for you your brother and your sister."

"I hope we're sitting in the front row," shouted Reese, "even if we do get wet!"

Try It
Write six sentences of our own. Write two sentences with series, two with direct addresses, and two with multiple adjectives.

1. _____

2. _____

3. _____

4. _____

5. _____

6. _____

Lesson 2.12 Commas: Combining Sentences (between clauses), Set-Off Dialogue

Simple sentences may become more interesting when they are combined into compound or complex sentences. Sometimes, this means using **commas**.

Use a comma to combine two independent clauses with a coordinate conjunction. The student must read three chapters, *and* answer the questions at the end of each chapter.

When combining an independent clause to a dependent clause (a complex sentence) use a comma. The clauses are connected with a comma and subordinate conjunction.

> *Although* the skies were sunny now, clouds were rolling in.

Commas are used when setting off dialogue from the rest of the sentence.

> The salesperson said, *"Our gym has classes in aerobics, kickboxing, and cycling."*

Match It

Draw an arrow to connect the sentences in Column A with the types of sentences in Column B.

Column A	Column B
I. Lisa asked, "What instrument do you play in the band?"	compound sentence
2. The distance is long, but the runner is strong.	complex sentence
3. Unless the movie is a comedy, I don't think I want to see it.	dialogue

---

4. "How much will it cost to remodel the kitchen?" the customer asked the contractor.	compound sentence
5. As long as the designs are good, the clothes will sell well.	complex sentence
6. The portrait is modern, yet it has an antique look.	dialogue

Lesson 2.12 Commas: Combining Sentences (between clauses), Set-Off Dialogue

Proof It
Proofread the following biography. Add or delete commas as necessary.

> _℮_ – **deletes incorrect letters, words, punctuation**
> ʌ – **inserts a comma**

Arthur Ashe

Arthur Ashe was born in Richmond, Virginia in 1943. He started playing tennis, when he was seven years old. Although the field was dominated by white athletes Ashe won many amateur titles in his teenage years. He won a scholarship to UCLA and during college competed in Wimbledon for the first time.

Ashe continued to win many major titles. In 1968 he won the U.S. Open becoming the top male ranked player in the United States Lawn Tennis Association. Until 1973 no African American had been permitted to compete in the South African tournament Ashe became the first. He went on to win Wimbledon and the World Championship of Tennis. He was the top ranked tennis player in the world in 1975.

A heart attack in 1979 forced him to retire in 1980. In 1988, Ashe suffered a devastating blow when he discovered he had contracted AIDS from a previous heart operation. Ashe was terminally ill, but he remained an active spokesperson for race relations and AIDS. Arthur Ashe died in February 1993.

Try It
Write three sentences with commas of your own: one in a compound sentence, one in a complex sentence, and one with a quotation.

_____

_____

_____

_____

_____

Lesson 2.13 Commas: Personal Letters and Business Letters

Commas are used in both personal and business letters.

Personal Letters
Commas appear in four of the five parts of the personal letter.

Heading:	2633 Lane Road
	Meridian, OH 30000
	June 3, 2008
Salutation:	Dear Kelly,
Body:	comma usage in sentences
Closing:	Your friend,

Business Letters
Commas appear in four of the six parts of the business letter.

Heading:	2200 Meridian Drive
	Riverside, CA 10000
	October 10, 2008
Inside Address:	Ms. Corrine Fifelski, Director
	Lakeview Sound Design
	907 Effington Boulevard
	Boulder, CO 20000
Body:	comma usage in sentences
Closing:	Sincerely,

Identify It
Read each line from a letter. If it is missing a comma, write an **X** on the line. If not, leave the line blank.

1. _____ 1473 Oliver Drive

2. _____ Dear Tiffany

3. _____ I went to the grocery store book store and shoe store.

4. _____ Your sister,

Lesson 2.13 Commas: Personal Letters and Business Letters

Rewrite It

Rewrite the following personal letter. Add all of the required commas in your rewrite.

---

927 Cobblestone Road
Buffalo NY 50000
September 3 2008

Dear Mimi

   How are you? I hope you had a great summer vacation. I saw something fantastic on my trip to visit my grandparents in Japan. Do you remember studying about World War II in history class? Well I got to see an actual living relic from World War II. In the middle of Tokyo there is a tree that was hit with a bomb. Remarkably, the tree survived! We saw lots of fascinating things on our trip through Japan, but the tree was my favorite. I can't wait to see you on your next trip to Buffalo and show you the pictures. I even brought you back a special souvenir, a *maneki neko* cat. This means *beckoning cat,* and it's a lucky charm in Japan.

Your friend

Akira

_____

_____

_____

_____

_____

_____

_____

_____

_____

_____

_____

_____

Lesson 2.14 Quotation Marks

Quotation marks are used to show the exact words of a speaker. The quotation marks are placed before and after the exact words.

> *"Let's go to the movies tonight,"* said Janice. *"The new action adventure was released."*

Quotation marks are also used when a direct quotation is made within a direct quotation. In this case, single quotation marks are used to set off the inside quotation.

> John said, "Miss Robinson clearly said, *'The project is due tomorrow.'*"

Single quotes express what Miss Robinson said. Double quotes express what John said.

Quotation marks are used with some titles. Quotation marks are used with the titles of short stories, poems, songs, and articles in magazines and newspapers.

> *"North Carolina Takes the Championship"* – newspaper article

If a title is quoted within a direct quotation, then single quotation marks are used.

> Melissa said, "Did you read the article *'Saving Our Oceans'* in the magazine?"

Identify It
On the lines, write a **DQ** for direct quote, a **QQ** for quote within quote, a **T** for title, and a **TQ** for title in quote.

1. _____ Sandra shouted, "Our team won the game!"

2. _____ Suzie responded, "I heard the coach say, 'This was my best team ever!'"

3. _____ The magazine <u>Sports Today</u> had an article called "A Winning Season."

4. _____ "What did the article 'A Winning Season' say about our team?" Sandra asked.

5. _____ "The writer of the article thinks we could win the championship," Suzie said.

6. _____ "He said, 'The team is strong offensively and defensively and could go all the way,'" continued Suzie.

7. _____ "This is so exciting," yelled Sandra.

8. _____ Suzie said, "Let's go check out our newspaper 'Community Times' and see what they had to say!

Lesson 2.14 Quotation Marks

Rewrite It
Rewrite the following list of famous quotations, adding quotation marks where they are needed.

1. Arthur Ashe said, From what we get, we can make a living; what we give, however, makes a life.

   _____

   _____

2. The most important thing is not to stop questioning, said Albert Einstein.

   _____

3. Mahatma Ghandi said, The weak can never forgive. Forgiveness is the attribute of the strong.

   _____

4. Although the world is full of suffering, it is full also of the overcoming of it, said Helen Keller.

   _____

   _____

Try It
Write two sentences of dialogue that include direct quotations by characters. Write two sentences that include a title. Write two direct quotations of your own.

_____

_____

_____

_____

_____

_____

Lesson 2.15 Apostrophes

Apostrophes are used in contractions, to form possessives, and to form plurals.

Contractions are shortened forms of words. The words are shorted by leaving out letters. Apostrophes take the place of the omitted letters.

he is = he's   can not = can't

Possessives show possession, or ownership. To form the possessive of a singular noun, add an apostrophe and an **s**.

I'll carry *Harry's* notebook.

To form the possessive of plural nouns ending in **s**, simply add the apostrophe. If the plural noun does not end in an **s**, add both the apostrophe and an **s**.

The *puppies'* guardians are very happy.
The *women's* team has won every game.

Match It

The sentences in Column A contain words with apostrophes. Match these sentences to the types of apostrophes used in Column B. Draw an arrow to make your match.

Column A	Column B
1. Felicia's jacket is in my car.	contraction
2. She's my best friend.	singular possessive
3. The men's shirts are on the second floor.	plural possessive ending in **s**
4. The girls' tickets are at the box office.	plural possessive not ending in **s**

Column A	Column B
5. The parents' cars lined the street.	contraction
6. Patty's blanket is nearly done.	singular possessive
7. The children's toys are in the toy box.	plural possessive ending in **s**
8. Teddy's got the presentation.	plural possessive not ending in **s**

Lesson 2.15 Apostrophes

Complete It
Complete the following sentences by circling the best answer in parentheses.

1. (I'll, Ill) make an appointment first thing in the morning.

2. (Sams', Sam's) bicycle is outside the library.

3. The (books', book's) covers are worn.

4. Do you see the (mooses's, moose's) beautiful antlers?

5. (Don't, Do'nt) turn onto Shipman St.; it's closed.

6. You can buy your (rabbits, rabbit's) food and toys at the shelter's retail shop.

7. We'll pick up our (children's, childrens's) toys.

8. We (shouldn't, should'nt) leave without our umbrellas.

9. Did you see the (movie's, movies) review?

10. The (boys', boy's) helmets are ready to be picked up.

Try It
Write a skit with three or more characters. Use at least three contractions and at least three singular possessive and three plural possessive.

_____

_____

_____

_____

_____

_____

_____

_____

_____

_____

_____

_____

Lesson 2.16 Colons

Colons are used to introduce a series, to set off a clause, for emphasis, in time, and in business letter salutations.

Colons are used to introduce a series in a sentence.
> My favorite vegetables include the following: *broccoli, red peppers, and spinach.*

Colons are sometimes used instead of a comma (in more formal cases) to set off a clause.
> The radio announcer said: *"The game is postponed due to torrential rains."*

Colons are used to set off a word or phrase for emphasis.
> The skiers got off of the mountain as they expected the worst: *an avalanche.*

Colons are used when writing the time.
> Is your appointment at 9:00 or 10:00?

Business letters use colons in the salutation.
> Dear Miss Massey:

Identify It
Identify why the colon is used in each sentence. Write an **S** for series, **C** for clause, **E** for emphasis, **T** for time, or **L** for letter.

1. _____ The teacher said to do the following: read two chapters, answer the questions following each chapter, and write a paragraph about what was read.

2. _____ My alarm goes off at 6:15 A.M.

3. _____ The coach gave us some tips: eat right and train hard.

4. _____ All of my hard training paid off when I saw the sign ahead: Finish.

5. _____ Dear Dr. Brooks:

6. _____ The host said: "Let's eat!"

7. _____ Maya decided to see the movie when the reviewer summed it up in one word: hysterical.

8. _____ The triathlon consisted of three events: swimming, biking, and running.

Lesson 2.16 Colons

Proof It
Proofread the following dialogue. Add colons where needed.

‸ – inserts colon

"Hurry up, Henry, it's almost 1100. We want to get to the animal shelter soon," shouted Mrs. Knapp.

"I'm glad we're adopting from a shelter, Mom. There are so many dogs, cats, and other animals who don't have homes," Henry said.

"You're right, Henry," said Mrs. Knapp. "There are many reasons to adopt from a shelter it saves animals' lives, the animals have all been seen by a vet, and the animals are spayed and neutered."

"I can't wait to see Ginger," said Henry, "and tell her she is coming home with us! The shelter director told me "I'm so glad you are adopting an older dog. Older pets need homes just like the little ones."

"Well, we better get going, Henry," said Mrs. Knapp. "It's almost 1115, and we need to pick up some dog toys on the way there!"

Try It
Write four sentences with colons: one that introduces a series, one used with a clause, one that expresses emphasis, and one used with time.

_____

_____

_____

_____

_____

_____

_____

Lesson 2.17 Semicolons

A **semicolon** is a cross between a period and a comma. Semicolons can be used to join two independent clauses, to separate clauses containing commas, and to separate groups which contain commas.

Semicolons join two independent clauses when a coordinate conjunction is not used.
> The city's sounds are loud; I love the excitement.

Semicolons are used to separate clauses when they already contain commas.
> After the sun sets, the lights come on; the city is beautiful at night.

Semicolons are also used to separate words or phrases that already contain commas.
> Billi's new apartment has a bedroom for her, her sister, and her brother; a laundry room; an exercise room; and a game room.

Rewrite It
Rewrite the following sentences adding semicolons where needed.

1. The insulation in the room wasn't very effective it was freezing.

   _____

   _____

2. Although we were relieved it didn't rain, we needed it a drought was upon us.

   _____

   _____

3. They needed equipment to start a business computer monitor printer and furniture, such as desks, chairs, and lamps.

   _____

   _____

4. Riana has the aptitude for science it is her favorite subject.

   _____

   _____

5. Since the opening is delayed, we'll shop on Tuesday I'm looking forward to it.

   _____

   _____

Lesson 2.17 Semicolons

Solve It
Look at the following pictures. The scenes depicted complete the sentences below. Write the conclusion to each sentence by interpreting and matching them to a picture. Remember to add semicolons where they are needed in your completed sentences. Rewrite the entire sentence.

1. _____ it soared beyond the clouds.

   _____

2. Although the score was tied, our team looked strong_____.

   _____

3. The movie had all of the right parts: actors who were _____

   action that was _____ and music that was

   _____.

   _____

   _____

Try It
Write a review of a movie you have seen or a book you have read. Include at least two of the following uses of semicolons: between independent clauses, to separate clauses that contain clauses, and to separate words that contain commas.

_____

_____

_____

_____

_____

Lesson 2.18 Hyphens

Hyphens are used to divide words, to create new words, and are used between numbers.

Use a hyphen to divide the word between syllables.
    beau-ti-ful   per-form

Do not divide one-syllable words with fewer than six letters.
    through   piece

Do not divide one letter from the rest of the word.
    event-ful   not: e-ventful

Divide syllables after the vowel if the vowel is a syllable by itself.
    come-dy   not: com-edy

Divide words with double consonants between the consonants.
    swim-ming   mir-ror

Hyphens can be used to create new words when combined with *self*, *ex*, and *great*.
    The pianist was self-taught.

Hyphens are used between numbers.
    twenty-one

Complete It
Choose the best word in parentheses to complete each sentence.

1. Next year I'll pick an (instru-ment, instr-ument) to play in the band.

2. Julia burned her (ton-gue, tongue) on the hot chocolate.

3. An (o-ceanographer, ocean-ographer) studies the oceans and the plants and animals that live in them.

4. My (ex-coach, excoach) won teacher of the year.

5. The glass holds (thirty two, thirty-two) ounces.

6. The students are raising money for their chosen (char-ity, chari-ty).

7. Armonite would like a (ch-air, chair) for her bedroom.

8. The clock seems to be (run-ning, runn-ing) fast.

9. Richard's (great aunt, great-aunt) bakes the best blackberry pie.

10. Her jersey number is (sixty-four, sixty four).

Lesson 2.18 Hyphens

Hyphenate It

One word in each fact is underlined. On the line following the fact, rewrite the word using a hyphen (as if it would appear at the end of a line.)

1. The <u>longest</u> one syllable word in the English language is "screeched."

   _____

2. "Dreamt" is the only English word that ends in the <u>letters</u> **mt**. _____

3. In the 18th and 19th centuries, doctors used <u>leaches</u>

   to treat headaches. _____

4. No two lions have the same pattern of <u>whiskers</u> in their muzzles.

   _____

5. Bats are the only <u>mammals</u> that can fly. _____

6. <u>Basketball</u> star Shaquille O'Neal wears size 22 shoes. _____

7. Ann Meyers was the first <u>female</u> player to sign a contract with an NBA team.

   _____

8. The average lifespan of a major <u>league</u> baseball is seven pitches. _____

Try It

Use a dictionary to look up two words with the prefix **ex-**, two words with the prefix **great-**, and two words with the prefix **self-**. Write a sentence for each.

1. _____

   _____

2. _____

   _____

3. _____

   _____

4. _____

   _____

5. _____

   _____

6. _____

   _____

NAME _____

Lesson 2.19 Parentheses

Parentheses are used to show supplementary material, to set off phrases in a stronger way than commas, and to enclose numbers.

Supplementary material is a word or phrase that gives additional information.
Theresa's mother *(the dentist)* will speak to our class next week.

Sometimes, words or phrases that might be set off with commas are set off with parentheses instead. It gives the information more emphasis for a stronger phrase.
Leo's apartment building, *the one with the nice window boxes,* was voted prettiest in the neighborhood.
Leo's apartment building *(the one with the nice window boxes)* was voted prettiest in the neighborhood.

Parentheses are also used to enclose numbers.
Jacklyn wants to join the track team because *(1)* it is good exercise, *(2)* she can travel to other schools and cities, and *(3)* she can meet new friends.

Match It
Match the sentences in Column A with the reason why parentheses are used in Column B. Draw an arrow to make your match.

Column A

1. When cooking rice, don't forget to (1) rinse the rice, (2) steam the rice, and (3) eat the rice!

2. The preliminary findings (announced yesterday) are important to the study.

3. The dinosaur bones (a huge discovery) can be seen in the museum.

Column B

supplementary material

set-off with emphasis

enclose numbers

---

4. The orientation (for freshman) is this weekend.

5. Mac must (1) wash the dishes, (2) do his homework, and (3) get ready for bed.

6. We're setting up our lemonade stand (the one that made $100 last summer) Memorial Day weekend.

supplementary material

set-off with emphasis

enclose numbers

Lesson 2.19 Parentheses

Rewrite It
Rewrite the following paragraph, adding parentheses where necessary.

Special Olympics

The Special Olympics were founded with the knowledge that people with intellectual disabilities can learn, participate, and enjoy sports. Eunice Kennedy Shriver started a day camp sports included for people with intellectual disabilities. Her sister was one of the first participants. She realized how important playing sports was to the people at her camps. In 1968, she organized the first International Special Olympics Games. One thousand athletes from 26 U.S. states and Canada participated. Today, both summer and winter World Games are held with over 1,800 athletes from more than 150 countries participating. Thousands support Special Olympics by coaching, volunteering, or cheering on the committed athletes. The games continue to grow and attract athletes from all over the world!

_____
_____
_____
_____
_____
_____
_____
_____
_____
_____
_____
_____
_____
_____

Try It
Write three sentences about your favorite sporting event, either as a participant or a spectator. Use each of the three types of parentheses in your sentence.

1. _____
2. _____
3. _____

Review Chapter 2 Lessons 2.7–2.19

Review: Periods: After Imperative Sentences, In Dialogue, In Abbreviations, In Initials, In Decimals, In Money; Question Marks, Exclamation Points

Putting It Together

Complete the following sentences by adding periods, question marks, and exclamation points where needed.

1. "Marsha," called A.J., "I heard you got your driver's license"

2. Washington DC is the capital of the United States.

3. The equivalent of 3 is $\frac{3}{10}$.

4. The customer asked, "What comes on the garden salad"

5. Wow That was the best movie I've ever seen

Review: Commas: In a Series, Multiple Adjectives, Between Clauses, In Business Letters

Add commas in the appropriate places in the business letter.

1151 Davidson Street
Chicago IL 40000
April 8 2008

Mrs. Jane Merrinan Director
City Community Center
1200 Adams Street
Chicago IL 30000

Dear Mrs. Merrinan:

    My name is A.J. Byington. I am interested in applying as a summer counselor at the Civic Community Center and as a part-time volunteer during the school year. I am a freshman at Northwest High School. My experience has included tutoring coaching and counseling students in elementary school. Your varied well-rounded programs interest me. I have included my activities list and references. I look forward to talking with you in the near future. Thank you for your time.

Sincerely

A.J. Byington

A.J. Byington

Review Chapter 2 Lessons 2.7–2.19

Review: Commas: In Direct Address, Set-Off Dialogue; Quotation Marks; Apostrophes; Colons; Semicolons; Hyphens; Parentheses

Putting It Together

Proof the following paragraphs by adding commas, quotation marks, apostrophes, colons, semicolons, hyphens, and parentheses where needed.

Sharon are you going to the community center after school? asked Susan.

Yes, Im going right after school to play some basketball our team is going to the tournament. My greatgrandpa is going to cheer me on, answered Sharon.

Im so glad we have a center, said Sharon. We learned in school about the very first community center. It was started by two very brave women Jane Addams and Ellen Gates Starr.

Susan responded, I dont think Ive heard of them.

They lived way back in the 1800s. Life in cities was not easy, Sharon continued. Thousands of people worked in factories even kids and received little money in return. Jane and Ellen both wanted to help people. They moved into one of the worst parts of town. They found a big house on Halstead Street. They rented it and turned it into the first community center Hall House. Hall House offered child care for working mothers eventually leading to kindergarten classes. After awhile, many classes were offered to people of all ages art, music, drama, cooking, science, math, and languages. The people of the city were finally brought together in a place where they could socialize, relax, and escape their working lives, responded Sharon. Many of the people who came to Hall House went on to lead successful lives who helped other people.

Well, Susan, said Sharon, today's game will be played in honor of Jane Addams and Ellen Gates Starr!

Lesson 3.1 Verbs: *rise, teach, wrote*

The **present tense** of a verb tells that the action is taking place now or continuously.

    I *rise* at 6:00 every morning.
    Rona and Michael both *teach* third grade.
    Mimi and Chuck *write* well for kindergartners.

The **past tense** of a verb tells that the action took place in the past.

    I *rose* at 6:30 yesterday morning.
    A substitute *taught* our English class this morning.
    Robyn *wrote* her descriptive paragraph at the coffee shop.

The **past participle** of a verb tells that the action began in the past and was completed in the past. In order to form the past participle, the verb must be preceded by one of the following verbs: *was, were, has, had,* or *have.*

    Rachel *had risen* every day at the same time, until she got the flu.
    Mrs. Khory *has taught* our English class in the past.
    Jean *has written* her paper four times and is still not satisfied with it.

Match It

Draw a line to match the sentences in Column A with the words they are missing in Column B.

Column A	Column B
1. Greg and Lisa _____ martial arts at the YMCA.	rise
2. My grandmother had _____ her recipe down before I even asked her.	rose
	risen
3. The sun has _____ a little earlier every morning.	teach
4. Mr. Lee had _____ at the same school for 30 years before he retired.	taught
5. I _____ a note for my mom and left it on the refrigerator.	taught
6. The sun _____ at 6:30 A.M. sharp.	write
7. Sasha _____ us how to double jump rope during recess yesterday.	wrote
8. Ryan and Jaime _____ nice poetry.	written
9. Kurt and Perry _____ at dawn.	

Lesson 3.1 Verbs: *rise, teach, wrote*

Complete It

Circle the correct usage of the verbs *rise, teach,* and *write.*

Much has been (written, wrote) about our world's waterways. Novelists and poets (written, wrote) about beautiful oceans, seas, and rivers. Some writers (risen, rise) at dawn for the inspiration a sunrise can bring. But our waterways may not always be that inspiring, unless we step in and do something about it.

The famous explorer Jacque Cousteau and many other conservationists have (taught, teach) us many lessons on ocean conservation. Our oceans and the marine life that inhabit them are at risk from many sources. Previous oil spills have (teach, taught) us that we must take safer measures when transporting oil.

Conservationists are people who take action to help protect the things they love. They (risen, rise) up and let their voices be heard. People who have (risen, rose) up in the past have noticed a change: a change for the better. New methods of oil transportation are being discussed, as well as oil clean-ups. Better ways to dispose of waste are being developed.

You can have your voice heard. You can (wrote, write) letters to government officials asking for better laws to save our waterways. You can volunteer to help clean trash and litter from oceans and rivers. One of the most important things you can do is (teach, taught) those around you about the importance of our oceans and marine life and how to keep them safe for everyone to enjoy for years and years to come.

Try It

Do you have a cause that is important to you? Write a letter to your local government official expressing your concerns. Include at least two of the verb forms from this lesson.

_____

_____

_____

_____

_____

_____

_____

Lesson 3.2 Verbs: *bring, take*

The irregular verbs *bring* and *take* are often confused with each other. When you *bring* something, it is coming in or toward you. When you *take* something, it is moving away.

The present tense of a verb tells that the action is taking place now or continuously.
> The teacher asked her students to *bring* in newspapers.
> The teacher asked her students to *take* books home.

The past tense of a verb tells that the action took place in the past.
> Jessica *brought* her books home.
> Jessica *took* magazines to her sick friend.

The past participle of a verb tells that the action began in the past and was completed in the past. In order to form the past participle, the verb must be preceded by one of the following verbs: *was, were, has, had* or *have*.
> He *had brought* the tickets over just before we left.
> He *had taken* the tickets to the game.

Complete It
Complete the following sentences by circling the best answers in parentheses.

1. Don't (bring, take) the library books out of the building.
2. Vicki and Anna (bring, brought) friends home every day after school.
3. Brian and Matt (take, taken) extra water to the baseball games.
4. Last year Lilly (bring, brought) cupcakes on her birthday.
5. Grover (brought, took) six cookies out of the box.
6. Yesterday, we (take, took) blankets and towels to the animal shelter.
7. The children were (bring, brought) home when it started to thunder.
8. Marv was (took, taken) to the hospital when he sprained his ankle.
9. Grandma said, "Aubrey, (bring, take) me a glass of water, please."
10. Charlie (brought, took) seeds from his own garden to plant new flowers in the park.

Lesson 3.2 Verbs: *bring, take*

Solve It
Choose the correct form of the verbs *bring* and *take* and complete the puzzle.

<u>Across</u>

2. Trisha had (brought, bring) everyone's favorite blueberry muffins to every meeting.

4. Adam and Mandy (take, bring) their puppy when they come for a visit.

5. Becky had (taken, take) flowers to the hospital every weekend for two years.

<u>Down</u>

1. Lisa and Dave (take, bring) meals to the elderly every evening.

2. Harold (brought, bring) his favorite book to read in the car.

3. Jake (bring, took) his cat to the vet for a check-up.

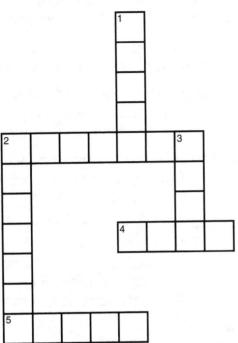

Try It
Write a letter to a friend or relative, using different forms of the verbs bring and take. Write about things that you either *bring* or *take* to or from school or home.

_____

_____

_____

_____

_____

_____

_____

_____

_____

_____

_____

_____

Lesson 3.3 Verbs: *lay, lie*

The irregular verbs *lay* and *lie* are easily confused.

The verb *lay* means *to place*.
The forms of the verb *lay* are *lay*, *laid*, and *laid*.

The verb *lie* means *to recline*.
The forms of the verb *lie* are *lie*, *lay*, and *lain*.

The present tense of a verb tells that the action is taking place now or continuously.
> The teachers *lay* the papers on their desks.
> The kittens *lie* by the window in the sun.

The past tense of a verb tells that the action took place in the past.
> Bobby *laid* his homework on the kitchen table.
> Yesterday, the kittens *lay* on the blankets in the laundry room.

The past participle of a verb tells that the action began in the past and was completed in the past. In order to form the past participle, the verb must be preceded by one of the following verbs: *was, were, has, had,* or *have*.
> Mother *has laid* her briefcase on the same table every night for years.
> The cats *have lain* in the same windowsill every evening.

Identify It

Write whether the forms of *lay* and *lie* mean *to place* or *to recline*. Write a **P** for *place* and an **R** for *recline*.

1. _____ Don't lie in the sun without sunscreen!

2. _____ It was unusual the papers were missing; he had laid them in the same spot every morning.

3. _____ Meagan and Ashley had lain in the sun too long.

4. _____ Jean laid the covers over the plates before the rain hit.

5. _____ Please lay the cups and plates at the end of the table.

6. _____ The toddlers lay down for a long nap earlier today.

7. _____ Don't lay your homework by your computer, you'll forget about it in the morning.

8. _____ Lie on the blanket on the sand.

9. _____ Barbara laid her blanket near the bed.

10. _____ Maggie lay down for a quick nap yesterday.

Lesson 3.3 Verbs: *lay, lie*

Complete It
Complete the following sentences by circling the best answers in parentheses.

1. Patrick has (laid, lain) on his arm too long and has lost feeling in it.

2. The exercisers (lay, lie) their towels in the basket on their way out.

3. I like to (lay, lie) down for a few minutes before dinner.

4. The writer (laid, lay) down his pen when he finished.

5. The same architects have (laid, lain) out the plans every year.

6. Mr. Shaloub has (laid, lain) out the homework assignments on the work table.

7. The sleeping turtle has (laid, lain) in the same spot for hours.

8. "Please (lay, lie) your homework assignments on my desk," said the teacher.

9. We poured club soda on the stain in the carpet and let it (lay, lie) for several minutes.

10. The picnickers (laid, lay) the lunch boxes on the tablecloth before the wind blew it away.

Try It
Write six sentences of your own. Write one sentence for each of the forms of *lie* and *lay*.

1. _____

2. _____

3. _____

4. _____

5. _____

6. _____

Lesson 3.5 Adjectives: *more* and *most;* *good/better/best; bad/worse/worst*

Comparative and **superlative adjectives** can also be formed by adding the words *more* (comparative) and *most* (superlative) before the adjective. The words *more* and *most* are used instead of adding the endings **-er** and **-est** to longer adjectives.

> The sunrise today was even **more** beautiful than the one yesterday.
> It was the **most** magnificent sunrise of any I'd ever seen.

The adjectives *good* and *bad* have their own rules.

> That was a *good* movie that we saw last night.
> It looks like there will even be a *better* one out next weekend.
> But neither will be the *best* movie of all time.
>
> Remove the *bad* apples from the basket.
> The *worse* of the two pies were made with bad apples.
> It was the *worst* pie I had ever eaten.

Identify It

Identify the following sentences by writing a **C** for comparative or an **S** for superlative.

1. _____ The alexandrite, June's birthstone, is one of the most rare gemstones.

2. _____ The red garnet, the birthstone of January, is more popular than the green garnet.

3. _____ The best peridots, the August birthstone, have a greenish-yellowish color.

4. _____ The most expensive color of sapphires, September's stone, is blue.

5. _____ Because of its color variety, tourmalines, the birthstone of October, have become more popular in recent years.

6. _____ A real aquamarine has much better quality than its synthetic substitute.

7. _____ Some of the most beautiful shades of purple are found in the February birthstone, amethyst.

8. _____ Fine emeralds, the birthstone of May, are more rare than fine diamonds.

9. _____ The most popular gemstone is the diamond, April's birthstone.

10. _____ The July birthstone, ruby, is known to celebrate the most special occasions.

11. _____ Most topaz, the November birthstone, come in many soft colors.

12. _____ The December birthstone, zircon, is one of the most recent additions to the list of common gems.

Lesson 3.5 Adjectives: *more* and *most;* *good/better/best; bad/worse/worst*

Rewrite It
Rewrite the following sentences, correcting the forms of the adjectives used.

1. Angie liked the red sweater best than the yellow one.

   _____

2. The living room was most decorative than the kitchen.

   _____

3. Jackie was the better runner on the whole team.

   _____

4. I waited to go shopping; that was the bad discount I had seen all week.

   _____

5. The race landed on the more humid day of the year.

   _____

6. This comedians monologue was worst than the one before.

   _____

7. Even though I didn't win, the day I competed in the race was a better day.

   _____

8. The letter came back; it must have been a worse address.

   _____

Try It
Write a paragraph comparing your school subjects to each other. Use at least four of the following words in your paragraph: *more, most, good, better, best, bad, worse, worst.*

_____

_____

_____

_____

_____

_____

_____

_____

Lesson 3.6 Adjectives and Adverbs: *bad/badly, good/well*; Adverb: *already* vs. Phrase: *all ready*

Adverbs modify verbs, adjectives, and other adverbs. Some adverbs are easily confused with adjectives.

Bad is an adjective, and *badly* is an adverb.

> That was a *bad* concert; the music was too loud. (*bad* modifies the noun *concert*)
>
> Tyler drives *badly*; he almost ran that stop sign. (*badly* modifies the verb *drives*)

Good is an adjective, and *well* is an adverb.

> We watched a *good* game. (*good* modifies the noun *game*)
>
> Both teams played *well*. (*well* modifies the verb *played*)

The word *already* is an adverb. It answers the question *when*.

> It was morning and *already* time to leave.

The phrase *all ready* means *completely ready*.

> The team was *all ready* to leave.

Complete It

Circle the correct word in parentheses. Then, underline the word it modifies (except for numbers 5 and 6) and write what part of speech it is on the lines after each sentence.

1. We threw out the (bad, badly) bruised orange. _____

2. Celina played (good, well) and won her match. _____

3. I just finished a really (good, well) book; I couldn't put it down. _____

4. The instructions were (bad, badly), and we got lost. _____

5. By the time the bus picked us up we were (all ready, already) late.

6. If everyone in the class is (all ready, already) to go, we'll line up at the door.

7. It was a (good, well) recipe; I'll make that again. _____

8. If our chorus sings (good, well), we'll advance to the semifinals. _____

9. Daryl (bad, badly) sang the last song. _____

10. Ally had a (bad, badly) excuse for not playing in the game. _____

Lesson 3.6 Adjectives and Adverbs: *bad/badly, good/well;*
Adverb: *already* vs. Phrase: *all ready*

Rewrite It

Rewrite the following letter, correcting the use of the words *bad, badly, good, well, all ready,* and *already* as necessary.

Dear Grandpa,

    I'm sorry you couldn't make it to my soccer game last Saturday. I played very good. Our team had been playing bad until a couple of weeks ago. We all got together and watched the World Cup on television. Teams from all over the world compete to determine a world champion. The United States' women's team played so good in the first Women's World Cup that they won the tournament. Our team had all ready lost several games when we watched the World Cup. We needed some well motivation. It worked. We won our next three games. Now, we're already to go to the championships.

                Love,
                Hannah

_____

_____

_____

_____

_____

_____

_____

_____

_____

_____

Try It

Write six sentences of your own. Write a sentence using each of the following words: *bad, badly, good, well, all ready, already.*

_____

_____

_____

_____

_____

_____

Lesson 3.7 Homophones: *cereal/serial, coarse/course, counsel/council*

Homophones are words that sound the same but have different spellings and different meanings. There are hundreds of homophones in the English language.

> *cereal* - food made from grain
> *serial* - of a series
>
> *coarse* - rough
> *course* - path; school subject
>
> *council* - a group of people who plans or makes laws
> *counsel* - advise

If you are unsure about which homophone to use, look up the meanings in a dictionary.

Identify It
Circle the correct homophone in each sentence.

1. My teacher will (council, counsel) me on what subjects to take next year.

2. This material has a smooth texture but that one is more (course, coarse).

3. The television program is going to be shown as a (cereal, serial); once a week for six weeks.

4. The (council, counsel) meets every Wednesday evening to discuss city plans.

5. I like to ride my bike on the scenic (course, coarse) along the river.

6. My favorite breakfast is a big bowl of (cereal, serial).

7. The (course, coarse) wallpaper adds more texture to the walls.

8. My coach will (council, counsel) me on how to train for the upcoming event.

9. Record the (cereal, serial) number of your new appliances.

10. I need to select one more (course, coarse) to take next semester.

11. She is going to propose the new law at the next (council, counsel) meeting.

12. Do you prefer oat, wheat, or rice (cereal, serial)?

13. My tax advisor can (council, counsel) me on the new codes.

14. The articles in the newspaper appear as a (cereal, serial) every Thursday.

15. I got a paper cut on that paper; I didn't realize it was so (course, coarse).

16. The golfers all agreed that this was a tough (course, coarse) to play.

17. The (council, counsel) agreed to pass the new law.

18. Sometimes I eat (cereal, serial) for dinner.

Lesson 3.7 Homophones: *cereal/serial, coarse/course, counsel/council*

Proof It
Proofread the following dialogue. Change the homophones as needed.

> *e* – deletes incorrect letters, words, punctuation
> ^ – inserts correct letters, words, punctuation

"Hey, Dad," exclaimed Russ, "I've decided what I want to be when I finish school."

"Oh, you have, have you," said Dad. "Sit down and eat your serial and tell me all about it."

"I want to work with dinosaurs. Well, at least what is left of them. I want to be a paleontologist," exclaimed Russ.

"Don't paleontologists study more than just dinosaurs? I think they also study ancient plants and microorganisms. You should have your teacher council you on the different areas you could pursue," suggested Dad.

"That's exactly what I plan to do," piped in Russ. "I'm going to meet with the school guidance counselor to discuss what courses I should take—probably lots of science and math. I heard there is a TV cereal about paleontology coming up soon."

"Well," continued Dad, "I think you have set a nice coarse for yourself. Now, I'm late for my counsel meeting."

Try It
Write a sentence for each of the homophones in this lesson. Be sure to use the correct homophone in each sentence.

_____

_____

_____

_____

_____

_____

Lesson 3.8 Homophones: *overseas/oversees, ring/wring, cent/scent/sent*

Homophones are words that sound the same but have different spellings and different meanings.

> *overseas* - abroad or beyond the sea
> *oversees* - supervises
>
> *ring* - a circular band; the sound of a bell
> *wring* - squeeze
>
> *cent* - one penny
> *scent* - odor
> *sent* - past tense of send

If you are unsure about which homophone to use, look up the meanings in a dictionary.

Match It
Fill in the blanks in the sentences in Column A with a homophone from Column B.

Column A	Column B
1. I bid one _____ more and won the item.	overseas
2. Deb has a beautiful _____ on her finger.	oversees
3. The sailor was stationed _____.	ring
4. The flowers have a beautiful _____.	wring
5. _____ out the dish cloth over the sink.	cent
6. Mr. Morgan _____ metal production.	scent
7. David _____ the envelope yesterday.	sent

8. My oldest dog _____ feeding time for all of my pets.	overseas
9. I would like to travel _____ for a semester.	oversees
10. It was raining so hard I had to _____ out my shirt.	ring
11. Did I hear someone _____ the doorbell?	wring
12. The letter was _____ to the wrong address.	cent
13. The item costs three dollars and one _____.	scent
14. The perfume has a strong _____.	sent

Lesson 3.8 Homophones: *overseas/oversees, ring/wring, cent/scent/sent*

Rewrite It
Rewrite the following postcard, correcting the incorrect homophones.

Dear Tiffany,

 I'm so glad I signed up for the semester oversees program. The fundraising was worth it. Switzerland is beautiful. We have learned a lot about their government and what the country produces. We even went to a chocolate factory and met the man who overseas the production of candy bars! The cent in the factory was wonderful! Switzerland is also known for its jewelry. I saw a beautiful wring in a shop window. From now on, I'm saving every sent so maybe I can come back someday. I scent an oversees package to you. It's not jewelry, but it is chocolaty! I can't wait to see you!

                              Your sister,
                              Kathryn

_____

_____

_____

_____

_____

_____

_____

_____

_____

_____

Try It
Write a sentence for each of the homophones from this lesson.

_____

_____

_____

_____

_____

_____

_____

Lesson 3.9 Contractions

A **contraction** is when two words are combined to make one word. An apostrophe is used to substitute for letters. Following are some examples of common contractions in their groups. Not every form is listed.

am	contraction		are	contraction
I am	I'm		you are	you're
			we are	we're
is, has	contraction		they are	they're
he is/has	he's			
it is/has	it's		**would, had**	contraction
what is/has	what's		I would/had	I'd
that is/has	that's		you would/had	you'd
here is/has	here's		she would/had	she'd
			we would/had	we'd
have	contraction			
I have	I've		**not**	contraction
you have	you've		can not	can't
we have	we've		do not	don't
they have	they've		is not	isn't
could have	could've		will not	won't
			should not	shouldn't
will	contraction		are not	aren't
I will	I'll		was not	wasn't
she will	she'll		has not	hasn't
it will	it'll		have not	haven't
we will	we'll			
			let	contraction
			let us	let's

Complete It

Complete the following sentences by writing the words in parentheses as contractions.

1. (I am) _____ hungry; when are we going to eat?

2. (Here is) _____ the hat that I lost last season.

3. (You have) _____ got to see this movie!

4. If you give the money to her, (she will) _____ buy the tickets for you.

5. (They are) _____ going to meet us at the game.

6. (We had) _____ been waiting for a table a long time when they called our name.

7. (Let us) _____ eat quickly.

8. We (do not) _____ have much time.

Lesson 3.9 Contractions

Match It
Draw a line to match the words in Column A with their contractions in Column B. These contractions are not on the list, but follow the same patterns.

Column A	**Column B**
1. she is or she has	might've
2. would have	they'll
3. might have	they'd
4. he will	weren't
5. they will	she's
6. he would or he had	hadn't
7. they would or they had	couldn't
8. could not	he'd
9. were not	would've
10. had not	he'll

Try It
Write a sentence for each of the contractions in the activity above. Be sure to use the contraction form of the words.

_____

_____

_____

_____

_____

_____

_____

_____

_____

_____

_____

Lesson 3.10 Negatives and Double Negatives

A **negative** sentence states the opposite. Negative words include *not, no, never, nobody, nowhere, nothing, barely, hardly,* and *scarcely;* and contractions containing the word *not.*

Double negatives happen when two negative words are used in the same sentence. Don't use double negatives; it will make your sentence positive again, and it is poor grammar.

Negative: We *won't* go anywhere without you.
Double Negative: We *won't* go *nowhere* without you.

Negative: I *never* like to ride my bike after dark.
Double Negative: I *don't never* like to ride my bike after dark.

Negative: I can *hardly* wait until baseball season.
Double Negative: I *can't hardly* wait until baseball season.

Rewrite It
Rewrite the following sentences. Correct the sentence if it contains a double negative.

1. I love breakfast; I can't imagine not skipping it.

_____

2. I can't scarcely believe I made it all the way down the slope without falling.

_____

3. Samantha doesn't never like to wear her coat outside.

_____

4. The class hasn't received their report cards yet.

_____

5. I'm not going nowhere until it stops raining.

_____

6. Paul has barely nothing to contribute to the argument.

_____

7. Sarah never reveals her secrets.

_____

8. I don't think nobody can make it to the event early.

_____

Lesson 3.10 Negatives and Double Negatives

Proof It
Proofread the following biography. Correct mistakes made with double negatives.

> *e* – deletes incorrect letters, words, punctuation
> ^ – inserts correct letters, words, punctuation

Jane Goodall

As a young girl, Jane Goodall knew she wanted to work with chimpanzees. She fulfilled her dream; although at the time (early 1960s) it was not scarcely common for women to work in Africa. At the time, nobody couldn't have dreamed of the success she would have with the chimpanzees of Tanzania. When the chimps first noticed Goodall in the forests, they didn't never stay close. Goodall didn't never give up.

Before this time, it was not believed by nobody that chimpanzees and other animals have personalities, but Goodall recorded proof. Goodall even witnessed one family of chimps adopt an orphan baby.

The Jane Goodall Institute for Wildlife Research, Education, and Conservation supports continuing study on wild chimpanzees. However, it is not hardly just about research. The institute promotes community-centered development programs and habitat protection efforts in Africa.

Try It
Write six negative sentences using each of the following words: *not, never, nobody, nowhere, nothing, barely, hardly,* and *scarcely.*

_____

_____

_____

_____

_____

Review Chapter 3 Lessons 1-10

Review: Verbs: *rise, teach, write*; Verbs: *bring, take*; Verbs: *lay, lie*

Putting It Together

Draw a line to match the sentences in Column A with their missing verbs in Column B.

Column A	**Column B**
1. The team had _____ early every day.	take
2. The organizations _____ us to respect the world.	wrote
3. The author _____ many novels.	risen
4. The couple has _____ their dog for a walk in the same park every day since he was a puppy.	laid
5. Mom asked Dad to _____ home some peaches.	teach
6. The kittens _____ on my homework at night.	lie
7. Don't forget to _____ back your library books.	bring
8. Janet _____ her jacket over the chair.	taken

Review: Adjectives: *busy/busier/busiest, early/earlier/earliest, easy/easier/easiest, more/most, good/better/best, bad/worse/worst*; Adjectives and Adverbs: *bad/badly, good/well*; Adverb: *already* vs. Phrase: *all ready*

Complete the following sentences by circling the best answer in parentheses.

1. We climbed the (more, most) enormous rock we had ever seen.

2. That was the (easy, easiest) game we have ever won.

3. With all of the Earth Day activities, Saturday is going to be a (busy, busiest) day.

4. I'd like to take part in the (earlier, earliest) of the two events, so I can finish sooner.

5. It was the (worse, worst) cereal I had eaten; it was much too sweet.

6. The (easy, easier) part of the two part assignment comes first.

7. This book was (more, most) interesting than that book.

8. It was a (bad, badly) purchase; we hadn't put enough thought into it.

9. If I'm the (early, earliest) one there, I'll be able to chose from the best activities.

10. They did not bake (good, well); they burned the muffins.

11. The documentary was (better, best) than the science fiction film.

12. It's early in the morning, and it's (all ready, already) hot.

Review Chapter 3 Lessons 1–10

Review: Homophones: *cereal/serial, coarse/course, council/counsel, overseas/oversees, ring/wring, cent/scent/sent*; Contractions; Negatives/Double Negatives

If the sentence correctly uses homophones, contractions, and double negatives, write a **C** on the line. If the sentence incorrectly uses homophones, contractions, or uses double negatives, write an **X** on the line. Then, write the word that would correctly complete the sentence.

1. Sydney likes raisins and granola in his cereal. _____ _____

2. That material was too course for Judy. _____ _____

3. The counsel meets twice a week. _____ _____

4. Mitzi's going overseas to visit her friends. _____ _____

5. Lynn bought herself a beautiful ring. _____ _____

6. Rebecca wouldn't even pay a sent for that material. _____ _____

7. The magazine articles Nathan's writing will be released as a cereal. _____
_____

8. Debbie ran on a beautiful tree-lined coarse around a lake. _____
_____

9. Greg will council his staff on the new project. _____ _____

10. Dr. Henry, the senior veterinarian, overseas the veterinary students. _____
_____

11. Please ring out the towels before placing them in the dryer. _____
_____

12. Stacy liked the sent of the flowers in the window box. _____ _____

13. Elizabeth cent in her application to the coffee shop. _____ _____

14. Le'ts stop for pizza after our ride. _____ _____

15. Our teacher told us to never stop learning. _____ _____

Lesson 4.1 Writer's Guide: Prewriting

The five steps of the writing process are **prewriting**, **drafting**, **revising**, **proofreading**, and **publishing**.

Prewriting, the first stage of the writing process, involves planning and organizing. This is the stage where you get the ideas for your paper and start plotting it out.

When you prewrite, you:

- Think of ideas for your topic that are not too narrow or too broad. Write down your chosen ideas.

- Select your favorite topic, the one you think you can write about the best.

- Write down anything that comes to your mind about your chosen topic. Don't worry about grammar and spelling at this stage. This is called *freewriting*.

- Organize your information the way you might organize it in your paper. Use a graphic organizer. Graphic organizers visually represent the layout and ideas for a written paper. Graphic organizers include spider maps, Venn diagrams, story boards, network trees, and outlines.

- Use your graphic organizer to find out what information you already know and what information you need to learn more about.

Prewriting Example

Assignment: biography of a hero

Topic ideas: Martin Luther King, Jr., Eleanor Roosevelt, Jesse Owens, Cleveland Amory, Lance Armstrong, Rachel Carson

Freewriting of selected topic: Cleveland Amory hero of animals. Author. Founder of the Fund for Animals. Wrote The Cat Who Came for Christmas. Read Black Beauty as a child and wanted a ranch for rescued animals. Established Black Beauty Ranch for rescued animals.

Graphic organizer:

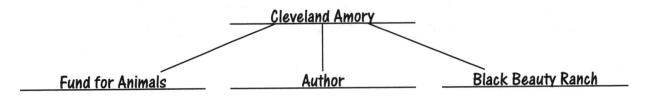

Lesson 4.2 Writer's Guide: Drafting

Drafting involves writing your rough draft. Don't worry too much about grammar and spelling. Write down all of your thoughts about the subject, based on the structure of your graphic organizer.

When you draft, you:

- Write an **introduction** with a topic sentence. Get your readers' attention by stating a startling statistic or asking a question. Explain the purpose of your writing.

- Write the **body** of your paper. Use your graphic organizer to decide how many paragraphs will be included in your paper. Write one paragraph for each idea.

- Write your **conclusion**. Your conclusion will summarize your paper.

Drafting Example

My hero was a hero: a hero to animals. Cleveland Amory (1917-1998) was an author, an animal advocate, and an animal rescuer. Reading <u>Black Beauty</u> as a child inspired a dream for Amory. Cleveland Amory made his dream a reality.

Amory founded The Fund for Animals. The Fund for Animals is an animal advocacy group that campaigns for animal protection. Amory served as its president, without pay, until his death in 1998. Cleveland Amory was an editor. He was an editor for <u>The Saturday Evening Post</u>. He served in World War II. After world war II, he wrote history books that studied society. He was a commentator on <u>The Today Show</u>, a critic for <u>TV guide</u>, a columnist for <u>Saturday Review</u>. Amory especially loved his own cat, Polar Bear, who inspired him to write three instant best-selling books: <u>The Cat Who Came for Christmas</u>, <u>The Cat and the Curmudgeon</u>, and <u>The Best Cat Ever</u>.

When Amory read <u>Black Beauty</u> as a child. When he read <u>Black Beauty</u>, he dreamed of place where animals could roam free and live in caring conditions. The dream is real at Black Beauty Ranch, a sanctuary for abused and abandoned animals The ranch's 1,620 acres serve as home for hundreds of animals, including elephants, horses, burros, ostriches, chimpanzees, and many more. Black Beauty Ranch takes in unwanted, abused, neglected, abandoned, and rescued domestic and exotic animals.

Cleveland Amory is my hero because he is a hero. He worked to make his dreams realities. His best-selling books, the founding of The Fund for Animals, and the opening of Black Beauty Ranch are the legacy of his dreams. Words from Anna Sewell's <u>Black Beauty</u>, the words that inspired Cleveland Amory, are engraved at the entrance to Black Beauty Ranch: "I have nothing to fear; and here my story ends. My troubles are all over, and I am at home." Cleveland Amory died on October 15, 1998. He is buried at Black Beauty Ranch, next to his beloved cat, Polar Bear.

Lesson 4.3 Writer's Guide: Revising

Revising is the time to stop and think about what you have already written. It is time to rewrite.

When you revise, you:

- Add or change words.
- Delete unnecessary words or phrases.
- Move text around.
- Improve the overall flow of your paper.

Revising Example (body of paper)

Cleveland Amory did more than just write about the animals he loved.

Amory founded The Fund for Animals. The Fund for Animals is an animal advocacy group that campaigns for animal protection. Amory served as its president, without pay, until his death in 1998. Cleveland Amory was an editor. He was an editor for The Saturday Evening Post. He served in World War II. After world war II he wrote history books that studied society. He was a commentator on The Today Show, a critic for TV guide, a columnist for Saturday Review. Amory especially loved his own cat, Polar Bear, who inspired him to write three instant best-selling books: The Cat Who Came for Christmas, The Cat and the Curmudgeon, and The Best Cat Ever.

Cleveland Amory made his childhood dream come true in 1979 when he opened Black Beauty Ranch in Texas.

When Amory read Black Beauty as a child. When he read Black Beauty, he dreamed of place where animals could roam free and live in caring conditions. The dream is real at Black Beauty Ranch, a sanctuary for abused and abandoned animals The ranch's 1,620 acres serve as home for hundreds of animals, including elephants, horses, burros, ostriches, chimpanzees, and many more. Black Beauty Ranch takes in unwanted, abused, neglected, abandoned, and rescued domestic and exotic animals.

(Revision annotations shown: "in 1967", "one of the world's most active", "rights and", "Amory extended his devotion to animals with Black Beauty Ranch.", "started his writing career as", "serving in", "Amory's love of animals, as well as great affection for", "led", "for hundreds of", "animals", and the letter "H")

Lesson 4.4 Writer's Guide: Proofreading

Proofreading is the time to look for more technical errors.

When you proofread, you:

- Check spelling.
- Check grammar.
- Check punctuation.

Proofreading Example (body of paper after revision)

Cleveland Amory started his writing career as an editor for <u>The Saturday Evening Post</u>. After serving in ~~w~~orld ~~w~~ar II, he wrote history books that studied society. He was a commentator on <u>The Today Show</u>, a critic for <u>TV ~~g~~uide</u>, a columnist for <u>Saturday Review</u>. Amory's love of animals, as well as great affection for his own cat, Polar Bear, led him to three instant best-selling books: <u>The Cat Who Came for Christmas</u>, <u>The Cat and the Curmudgeon</u>, and <u>The Best Cat Ever</u>.

Cleveland Amory did more than just write about the animals he loved. Amory founded The Fund for Animals in 1967. The Fund for Animals is one of the world's most active animal advocacy group~~s~~ that campaigns for animal rights and protection. Amory served as its president, without pay, until his death in 1998. Amory extended his devotion to animals with Black Beauty Ranch.

Cleveland Amory made his childhood dream come true in 1979 when he opened Black Beauty Ranch in Texas. He dreamed of ~~a~~ place where animals could roam free and live in caring conditions. The dream is real for hundreds of unwanted, abused, neglected, abandoned, and rescued domestic and exotic animals at Black Beauty Ranch. The ranch's 1,620 acres serve as home for elephants, horses, burros, ostriches, chimpanzees, and many more animals.

Lesson 4.5 Writer's Guide: Publishing

Publishing is the fifth and final stage of the writing process. Write your final copy and decide how you want to publish your work. Here is a list of some ideas:

- Read your paper to family and classmates.

- Illustrate and hang class papers in a "Hall of Fame" in your class or school.

- Publish your work in a school or community newspaper or magazine.

Publishing (compare to the other three versions to see how it has improved)

Biography of a Hero: Cleveland Amory

My hero was a hero: a hero to animals. Cleveland Amory (1917-1998) was an author, an animal advocate, and an animal rescuer. Reading <u>Black Beauty</u> as a child inspired a dream for Amory. Cleveland Amory made his dream a reality.

Cleveland Amory started his writing career as an editor for <u>The Saturday Evening Post</u>. After serving in World War II, Amory wrote history books that studied society. He was a commentator on <u>The Today Show</u>, a critic for <u>TV Guide</u>, and a columnist for <u>Saturday Review</u>. Amory's love of animals, as well as great affection for his own cat Polar Bear, led him to three instant best-selling books: <u>The Cat Who Came for Christmas</u>, <u>The Cat and the Curmudgeon</u>, and <u>The Best Cat Ever</u>.

Cleveland Amory did more than just write about the animals he loved. Amory founded The Fund for Animals in 1967. The Fund for Animals is one of the world's most active animal advocacy groups that campaigns for animal rights and protection. Amory served as its president, without pay, until his death in 1998. Amory extended his devotion to animals with Black Beauty Ranch.

Cleveland Amory made his childhood dream come true in 1979 when he opened Black Beauty Ranch in Texas. He dreamed of a place where animals could roam free and live in caring conditions. The dream is real for hundreds of unwanted, abused, neglected, abandoned, and rescued domestic and exotic animals at Black Beauty Ranch. The ranch's 1,620 acres serve as home for elephants, horses, burros, ostriches, chimpanzees, and many more animals.

Cleveland Amory is my hero because he is a hero. He worked to make his dreams realities. His best-selling books, the founding of The Fund for Animals, and the opening of Black Beauty Ranch are the legacy of his dreams. Words from Anna Sewell's <u>Black Beauty</u>, the words that inspired Cleveland Amory, are engraved at the entrance to Black Beauty Ranch: "I have nothing to fear; and here my story ends. My troubles are all over, and I am at home." Cleveland Amory died on October 15, 1998. He is buried at Black Beauty Ranch, next to his beloved cat, Polar Bear.

Lesson 4.6 Writer's Guide: Evaluating Writing

When you are evaluating your own writing and the writing of others, being a critic is a good thing.

You can learn a lot about how you write by reading and rereading papers you have written. As you continue to write, your techniques will improve. You can look at previous papers and evaluate them. How would you change them to improve them knowing what you know now?

You can also look at the writing of others: classmates, school reporters, newspaper and magazine writers, and authors. Evaluate their writing, too. You can learn about different styles from reading a variety of written works. Be critical with their writing. How would you improve it?

Take the points covered in the Writer's Guide and make a checklist. You can use this checklist to evaluate your writing and others' writing, too. Add other items to the checklist as you come across them or think of them.

Evaluation Checklist

❑ Write an introduction with a topic sentence that will get your readers' attention. Explain the purpose of your writing.

❑ Write the body with one paragraph for each idea.

❑ Write a conclusion that summarizes the paper, stating the main points.

❑ Add or change words.

❑ Delete unnecessary words or phrases.

❑ Move text around.

❑ Improve the overall flow of your paper.

❑ Check spelling.

❑ Check grammar.

❑ Check punctuation.

❑ _____

❑ _____

❑ _____

Lesson 4.7 Writer's Guide: Writing Process Practice

The following pages may be used to practice the writing process.

Prewriting

Assignment: _____

_____

Topic ideas: _____

_____

_____

Freewriting of selected topic: _____

_____

_____

_____

_____

_____

_____

_____

_____

_____

_____

_____

Graphic Organizer:

Lesson 4.7 Writer's Guide: Writing Process Practice

Drafting

_____

_____

_____

_____

_____

_____

_____

_____

_____

_____

_____

_____

_____

_____

_____

_____

_____

_____

_____

_____

_____

_____

_____

_____

_____

_____

_____

_____

Lesson 4.7 Writer's Guide: Writing Process Practice

Revising

_____

_____

_____

_____

_____

_____

_____

_____

_____

_____

_____

_____

_____

_____

_____

_____

_____

_____

_____

_____

_____

_____

_____

_____

_____

_____

_____

_____

Lesson 4.7 Writer's Guide: Writing Process Practice

Proofreading

_____

_____

_____

_____

_____

_____

_____

_____

_____

_____

_____

_____

_____

_____

_____

_____

_____

_____

_____

_____

_____

_____

_____

_____

_____

_____

Lesson 4.7 Writer's Guide: Writing Process Practice

Publishing

Final Draft: Include illustrations, photographs, graphic aids, etc.

_____

_____

_____

_____

_____

_____

_____

_____

_____

_____

_____

_____

_____

_____

_____

_____

_____

_____

_____

_____

_____

_____

_____

_____

Page 6

Common nouns name people, places, and things. They are general nouns (not specific). In a sentence, the noun is the person, place, or thing that can act or be acted upon.

teacher — a person
I like my *teacher*.

country — a place
I will visit another *country*.

book — a thing
What is your favorite *book*?

Proper nouns name specific people, places, and things.
Mrs. Crane — a specific person
Mrs. Crane is my favorite teacher.

United States of America — a specific place
I was born in the *United States of America*.

Animal Farm — a specific thing
Animal Farm is one of my favorite books.

Complete It
Use the word box below to complete the following sentences. Remember, common nouns are general and proper nouns are more specific. Proper nouns are also capitalized.

doctor	poem	song
Saturn	Dr. Green	planet
"Twinkle, Twinkle Little Star"		Where the Sidewalk Ends

1. I am writing a _____ song _____ for music class.
2. I took my cat to see _____ Dr. Green _____ when he had a cold.
3. The planet with the rings is called _____ Saturn _____.
4. My mom takes me to the _____ doctor _____ when I m sick.
5. My _____ poem _____ came in third place in the poetry contest.
6. Mars is the closest _____ planet _____ to the earth.
7. _Where the Sidewalk Ends_ is one of my favorite books.
8. My little sister likes to sing _Twinkle, Twinkle Little Star_ before she goes to bed.

Page 7

Proof It
Correct the mistakes in the use of common and proper nouns using proofreading marks.

/	— lowercase letter
≡	— capitalize letter
^	— insert words or letters

John Muir

John muir was born in 1838 in dunbar, Scotland. From a very young age, he had a love of Nature. He traveled all over the world. He came to the united states to observe nature and take notes on what he saw. He wrote many nature Books. John Muir was concerned for the welfare of the land. He wanted to protect it. He asked president Theodore roosevelt for help. The National parks System was founded by John Muir. This System sets aside land for Parks. The first national park was yellowstone national park. John Muir is also the founder of the sierra Club. The people in this Club teach others about nature and how to protect it. John Muir is known as one of the world s greatest conservation leaders.

Try It
Write a biography about someone you think is a hero. Use at least six common and six proper nouns correctly in your biography.

Answers will vary.

Page 9

Try It
Use the lines to explain how the nouns were made into their plural forms. The first one is done for you.

Column A	Column B	
match	matches	If the noun ends in ch, add an es.
eyebrow	eyebrows	Most nouns add an s.
volcano	volcanoes	If the noun ends in o with a consonant before the o, add es.
wolf	wolves	If the noun ends in an f or fe and has the v sound, change the f to v and add es.
trophy	trophies	If the noun ends in y, change the y to i and add es.
toothbrush	toothbrushes	If the noun ends in sh, add an es.
fax	faxes	If the noun ends in x, add an es.
sheriff	sheriffs	If the noun ends in an f or fe and has the f sound, add an s.
studio	studios	If the noun ends in o with a vowel before the o, add s.
kiss	kisses	If the noun ends in s, add an es.

Page 10

Irregular plural nouns do not have a pattern for changing from singular to plural. These nouns and their plural spellings have to be learned.

Singular noun:	Plural noun:
child	children
foot	feet
tooth	teeth

Some irregular nouns do not change at all when they are in the plural form. These forms also have to be learned.

Singular noun:	Plural noun:
fish	fish
deer	deer
moose	moose

The best way to learn these plural forms is by reading, writing, and practicing. Sometimes, when you read or hear these words used incorrectly, you will be able to tell if they are spelled incorrectly.

Find It
Write the irregular plural noun form of the following singular nouns on the lines provided. Use a dictionary if you need help.

1. ox _____ oxen _____
2. trout _____ trout _____
3. man _____ men _____
4. series _____ series _____
5. axis _____ axes _____
6. mouse _____ mice _____
7. sheep _____ sheep _____
8. salmon _____ salmon _____
9. woman _____ women _____
10. crisis _____ crises _____
11. oasis _____ oases _____
12. radius _____ radii _____

Answer Key

Page 11

Proof It
Correct the mistakes in the use of plural nouns using proofreading marks.

— delete words or letters
^ — insert words or letters

Have you ever thought about what happens to injured mice, ~~geese~~ *geese*, deer, mooses, or other wildlife when they are sick or injured? If they are lucky, they might be found by someone who knows about wildlife rehabilitation centers. Wildlife rehabilitation centers are places that care for sick or injured wild animals. They care for the animals until they can be released back into the wild. Sometimes, they take care of farm animals, too. This might include *oxen* ~~axes~~ or sheeps. Even species of fishes, like trout, salmon, and codes can be cared for and nursed back to health. Wildlife rehabilitation centers are wonderful places greatly needed by communities, especially as our cities extend farther into the wild. You can visit these centers and learn more about them.

You might even want to volunteer!

Try It
Write a fictional paragraph using as many of the irregular plural nouns on pages 10 and 11 as you can.

Answers will vary.

Page 12

A **pronoun** is a word used in place of a noun.

A **subject pronoun** can be the subject of a sentence.
I, you, he, she, and *it* are subject pronouns.
I found the ball.   *You* found the ball.
He found the ball.   *She* found the ball.
It is my favorite sport.

An **object pronoun** can be the object of a sentence.
Me, you, him, her, and *it* are object pronouns.
Matt gave the ball to *me*.   Matt gave the ball to *you*.
Matt gave the ball to *him*.   Matt gave the ball to *her*.
Matt threw *it*.

Possessive pronouns show possession.
My, mine, your, yours, his, her, hers, and *its* are possessive pronouns.
Anna gave *my* ball to Matt.
Anna gave *mine* to Matt. (includes the word ball)

The plural forms of personal pronouns include:
Subject: *we, you, they*   *We/You/They* found the ball.
Object: *us, you, them*   Matt gave the ball to *us/you/them*.
Possessive: *our, ours, your, yours, their, theirs*
Matt gave *our* ball/*ours*/*your* ball/*yours*/*their* ball/*theirs* to Anna.

Complete It
Complete the following sentences by choosing the best word in parentheses. Then, write what type of pronoun (subject, object, or possessive) it is on the line after the sentences.

1. __I__ (I, Me) like movies. ____subject____
2. Gloria handed the flowers to __her__ (his, her) sister. ____possessive____
3. Stephanie wanted __him__ (him, he) to ask her to the dance. ____object____
4. The teacher gave John __His__ (his, her) paper back. ____possessive____
5. __It__ (It, You) is the team's favorite food. ____subject____
6. __You__ (Him, You) are the quarterback on the football team. ____subject____
7. The teacher wanted __me__ (me, he) to try out for the play. ____object____
8. __She__ (Her, She) likes volleyball better than softball. ____subject____

Page 13

Identify It
The following skit contains subject, object, and possessive plural pronouns. Identify what each boldfaced plural pronoun is replacing on the line. Then, write whether the pronoun is a subject, object, or possessive on the line. The first one has been done for you.

Matt and Anna are on **their** ____Matt and Anna, possessive____ way to the park to play. On the way, **they** __Matt and Anna, subject__ meet Andrew and Stephanie.

We __Matt and Anna, subject__ are on our __Matt and Anna, possessive__ way to the park, said Matt. Can **you** __Andrew and Stephanie, subject__ join **us** __Matt and Anna, object__ ?

Can **we** __Andrew and Stephanie, subject__ play with **your** __Matt and Anna, possessive__ ball? asked Stephanie. **Ours** __Andrew and Stephanie, possessive__ is missing.

Yours __Andrew and Stephanie, possessive__ is missing? That's too bad, said Anna. Sure, **you** __Andrew and Stephanie, subject__ can play with **our** __Matt and Anna, possessive__ ball.

Matt, Anna, Andrew, and Stephanie all walked to the park. They would all play together.

I'll throw the ball to you, said Matt to Andrew. Then you can throw the ball to **them** __Anna and Stephanie, object__, Matt said pointing to Anna and Stephanie.

Hey, yelled Anna. I see a ball ahead. Could it be Andrew and Stephanie's ball?

Yes, it could be **their** __Andrew and Stephanie, possessive__ ball, answered Matt. Matt showed Andrew and Stephanie the ball. Sure enough, it was **theirs** __Andrew and Stephanie, possessive__

Page 14

A pronoun is a word used in place of a noun. Pronouns can be a subject, object, or possessive of the sentence. Pronouns can also be demonstrative.

Demonstrative pronouns replace nouns without naming the noun.
this   that   these   those

This is fun. (refers to an event or experience, for example a roller coaster)
That was wonderful. (refers to an event or experience, for example a movie)
These are good. (refers to a basket of apples)
Those are better. (refers to a barrel of pears)

This and *these* are usually used when the person or object is closer to the writer and speaker. *That* and *those* are usually used when the person or object is farther away from the writer or speaker.

This is fast (the roller coaster here), but *that* is faster (the roller coaster over there).
These look good (the apples in the basket that is close), but *those* look better (the pears in the barrel across the room).

Demonstrative pronouns, like other pronouns, add variety to your writing and speaking.

Match It
Draw a line to match the demonstrative pronoun in Column A with the objects of the sentence in Column B.

Column A   **Column B**
this   many newspapers across the room
that   one magazine at the library
these   one wallet in a pocket
those   many pencils on the desk

this   many ants on the ground
that   one book on the shelf
these   many bananas at the store
those   one experience at a baseball game

Spectrum Language Arts
Grade 6
150

Answer Key

Answer Key

Proof It

Proof the following dialogue. Use the proofreading marks in the key to delete the demonstrative pronouns that are incorrect and insert the correct words.

| ✁ — deletes incorrect word |
| ^ — inserts correct word |

    Lauren and Devin like shopping at the mall. But sometimes they can be hard

to please.

    Lauren, look at ~~these~~ these! (holding up earrings next to her ears)

    Devin sighed, I like ~~this~~ those better. (pointing to earrings on a counter farther away)

    Maybe I don t want earrings at all, said Lauren. What about ~~these~~ this? (waving

her arm in the air to display a bracelet)

    No, said Devin. Now, ~~those~~ that is perfect! (pointing to a belt hanging on the

far wall)

    Devin, look at ~~those~~ that (pointing to a clock on the wall) I think the store is closing,

cried Lauren.

    Yes, and ~~these~~ this (pointing to the price tag on the belt) won t make my mom very

happy, said Devin.

    Come on, replied Lauren. Let's come back again tomorrow!

Try It

Write more dialogue about Lauren and Devin s trip to the mall the next day. Be sure to use all four demonstrative pronouns: *this, that, these,* and *those.*

> Answers will vary.

15

A pronoun is a word used in place of a noun. Pronouns can be the subject, the object, or the possessive of a sentence.

Relative pronouns are pronouns that are related to nouns that have already been stated. They combine two sentences that share a common noun.

        who   whose   that   which

    The woman, *who* is a doctor, wasn t at the party.
    Who refers to the noun *woman.*

    The parents, *whose* children were at the party, were ready to go.
    Whose refers to the noun *parents.*
    (This relative pronoun shows possession).

    The note *that* you read is incorrect.
    That refers to the noun *note.*

    The newspaper articles, *which* are long, must be cut.
    Which refers to the noun *newspaper articles.*

Complete It

Complete the following sentences by choosing the correct relative pronoun in parentheses. Circle the correct answer.

1. Someone (who) that) likes kiwi usually likes strawberries.
2. Bicyclers (which (whose) bikes are ready can go to the starting line.
3. He likes movies (which (that) have a lot of action.
4. The man, (who) whose) lives across the street, is an actor.
5. The car (who (that) you drove is blocking the driveway.
6. The bananas, (which) that) are the ripest, are used in the recipe.

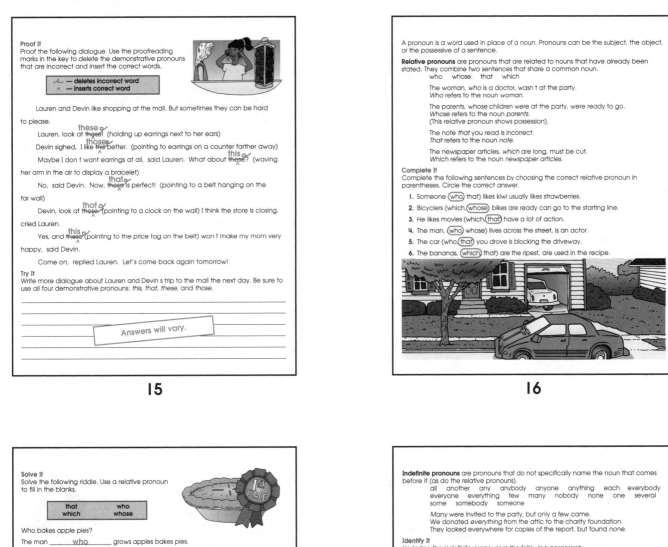

16

Solve It

Solve the following riddle. Use a relative pronoun to fill in the blanks.

| that | who |
| which | whose |

Who bakes apple pies?

The man _____who_____ grows apples bakes pies.

Who makes the best apple pies?

The man _____whose_____ apples are the sweetest bakes the best pies.

What didn t get baked into the pie?

The apple _____that_____ had a bruise did not go in the pie.

What won the prize?

The pies, _____which_____ were the sweetest, won the prize.

Try It

Try writing a riddle of your own. Follow the example above. Ask questions that require an answer with a relative pronoun. Use each relative pronoun at least once.

> Answers will vary.

17

Indefinite pronouns are pronouns that do not specifically name the noun that comes before it (as do the relative pronouns).

        all   another   any   anybody   anyone   anything   each   everybody
        everyone   everything   few   many   nobody   none   one   several
        some   somebody   someone

    Many were invited to the party, but only a few came.
    We donated *everything* from the attic to the charity foundation.
    They looked everywhere for copies of the report, but found *none.*

Identify It

Underline the indefinite pronouns in the following paragraph.

    The fair was approaching. <u>Each</u> of the cooks in town made ice cream cones for the fair. The cooks were put in pairs. <u>One</u> made the ice cream while <u>another</u> made the cones. You wouldn t think there would be any problems. However, there were <u>some</u>. <u>One</u> wanted the same flavor. <u>Another</u> wanted cherry. <u>Someone</u> wanted chocolate. <u>Several</u> even ate two scoops. That means <u>someone</u> had <u>none</u>. <u>Everyone</u> would think that is unfair. But the cooks were ready for <u>anything</u>. They made snow cones and <u>everybody</u> ate those instead. What else could happen? The sun melted the ice cream and the snow cones. Cooks quickly handed napkins to <u>everyone</u> with ice cream or snow cones. Then, they made milkshakes. <u>Everything</u> turned out fine.

18

Spectrum Language Arts
Grade 6

Answer Key

Rewrite It
Rewrite the following school news report. Replace the underlined words with indefinite pronouns. More than one answer is acceptable in many sentences.

The whole community attended the fundraiser for the school. The bake sale was a big success. Not a single item was left at the end of the evening. Chris and his friends looked for more brownies. The whole Carson family went home with something. Most of the students enjoyed the food, music, and art. Almost all of the student art pieces were purchased. Six or seven of the attendees want to help with next year s fundraiser.

Answers will vary.

Try It
Write a story about a recent gathering, like a family picnic or birthday party. Use at least eight indefinite pronouns. Underline each of them.

Answers will vary.

19

A **verb** is a word that tells the action or the state of being of a sentence. In this sentence, *walk* is the verb. It tells the action of the sentence.
The students *walk* home.

In this sentence, *shared* is the verb. It tells the action of the sentence.
Kevin *shared* his cake with Carol at the party last night.

In the first sentence the action is taking place now. In the second sentence the action took place in the past. Add **ed** to the present tense of a **regular verb** to make it past tense. If the word already ends in the letter **e**, just add the letter **d**.

Complete It
Write each word in present tense in the first sentence and then in past tense in the second sentence.

1. act	Today, I	act	Yesterday, I	acted
2. mend	Today, I	mend	Yesterday, I	mended
3. cook	Today, I	cook	Yesterday, I	cooked
4. bake	Today, I	bake	Yesterday, I	baked
5. answer	Today, I	answer	Yesterday, I	answered
6. cycle	Today, I	cycle	Yesterday, I	cycled
7. wave	Today, I	wave	Yesterday, I	waved
8. scream	Today, I	scream	Yesterday, I	screamed
9. bike	Today, I	bike	Yesterday, I	biked
10. jump	Today, I	jump	Yesterday, I	jumped
11. mow	Today, I	mow	Yesterday, I	mowed
12. yell	Today, I	yell	Yesterday, I	yelled
13. rake	Today, I	rake	Yesterday, I	raked
14. whisper	Today, I	whisper	Yesterday, I	whispered
15. divide	Today, I	divide	Yesterday, I	divided

20

Proof It
Proofread the following announcement. Use the proofreading marks to correct mistakes with the present and past tense forms of verbs and insert the correctly spelled words. Not all of the verbs are from this lesson.

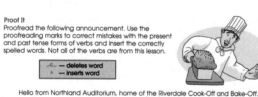
— deletes word
∧ — inserts word

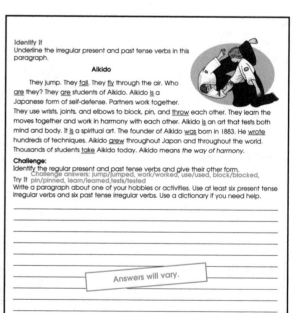

Hello from Northland Auditorium, home of the Riverdale Cook-Off and Bake-Off. The chefs are ready for the bake-off. The chefs cook meals last night. [cooked] The judges award [awarded] prizes for the best meals last night. The chefs baked today. Early this morning, the judges call the chefs over. [called] They talk with them about their recipes. [talked] The judges will now observe the baking. Judge Wilson and Judge Boggs looked over many of the cooks [look] shoulders. They laughed. It must be good news. I don t think they would joked if it [laugh] weren t. Two cooks answered a question for the judges. They act nervous. The judges [answer] tasted all of the baked goods. What will win the blue ribbon? Will cookies, cakes, [taste] brownies, or candy captured the top prize? The judges now handed a note to the announcer. The winner is .

Try It
Write a first-hand account of a school event. Include both present and past tense regular verbs.

Answers will vary.

21

Identify It
Underline the irregular present and past tense verbs in this paragraph.

Aikido

They jump. They <u>fall</u>. They <u>fly</u> through the air. Who <u>are</u> they? They <u>are</u> students of Aikido. Aikido <u>is</u> a Japanese form of self-defense. Partners work together. They use wrists, joints, and elbows to block, pin, and <u>throw</u> each other. They learn the moves together and work in harmony with each other. Aikido <u>is</u> an art that tests both mind and body. It <u>is</u> a spiritual art. The founder of Aikido <u>was</u> born in 1883. He <u>wrote</u> hundreds of techniques. Aikido <u>grew</u> throughout Japan and throughout the world. Thousands of students <u>take</u> Aikido today. Aikido means *the way of harmony*.

Challenge:
Identify the regular present and past tense verbs and give their other form.
Challenge answers: jump/jumped, work/worked, use/used, block/blocked pin/pinned, learn/learned, tests/tested
Try It
Write a paragraph about one of your hobbies or activities. Use at least six present tense irregular verbs and six past tense irregular verbs. Use a dictionary if you need help.

Answers will vary.

23

Answer Key

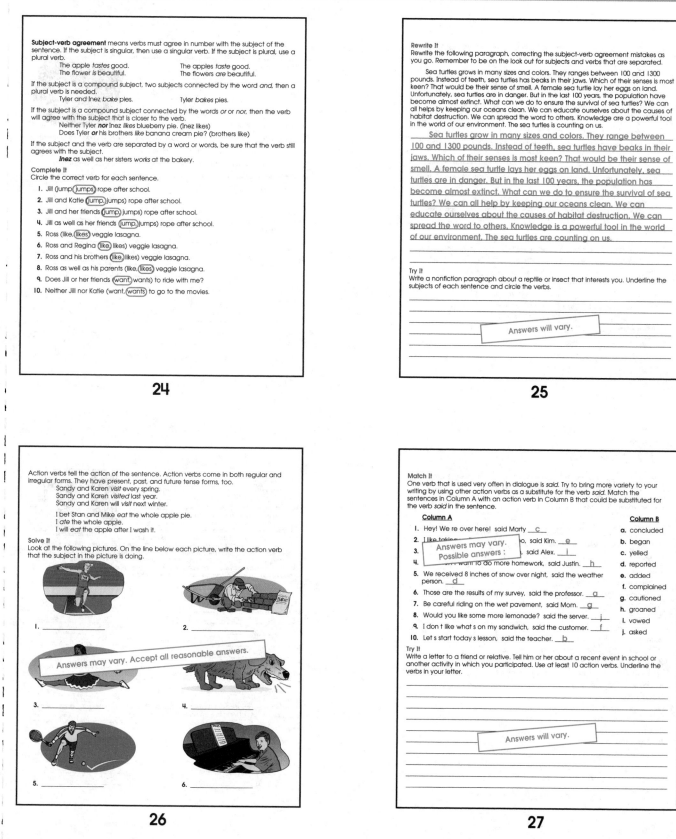

Page 24

Subject-verb agreement means verbs must agree in number with the subject of the sentence. If the subject is singular, then use a singular verb. If the subject is plural, use a plural verb.

The apple *tastes* good.　　　　The apples *taste* good.
The flower *is* beautiful.　　　　The flowers *are* beautiful.

If the subject is a compound subject, two subjects connected by the word *and*, then a plural verb is needed.

Tyler and Inez *bake* pies.　　　　Tyler *bakes* pies.

If the subject is a compound subject connected by the words *or* or *nor*, then the verb will agree with the subject that is closer to the verb.

Neither Tyler *nor* Inez *likes* blueberry pie. (Inez likes)
Does Tyler *or* his brothers *like* banana cream pie? (brothers like)

If the subject and the verb are separated by a word or words, be sure that the verb still agrees with the subject.

Inez as well as her sisters *works* at the bakery.

Complete It
Circle the correct verb for each sentence.

1. Jill (jump, **jumps**) rope after school.
2. Jill and Katie (**jump**, jumps) rope after school.
3. Jill and her friends (**jump**, jumps) rope after school.
4. Jill as well as her friends (**jump**, jumps) rope after school.
5. Ross (like, **likes**) veggie lasagna.
6. Ross and Regina (**like**, likes) veggie lasagna.
7. Ross and his brothers (**like**, likes) veggie lasagna.
8. Ross as well as his parents (like, **likes**) veggie lasagna.
9. Does Jill or her friends (**want**, wants) to ride with me?
10. Neither Jill nor Katie (want, **wants**) to go to the movies.

Page 25

Rewrite It
Rewrite the following paragraph, correcting the subject-verb agreement mistakes as you go. Remember to be on the look out for subjects and verbs that are separated.

Sea turtles grows in many sizes and colors. They ranges between 100 and 1300 pounds. Instead of teeth, sea turtles has beaks in their jaws. Which of their senses is most keen? That would be their sense of smell. A female sea turtle lay her eggs on land. Unfortunately, sea turtles are in danger. But in the last 100 years, the population have become almost extinct. What can we do to ensure the survival of sea turtles? We can all helps by keeping our oceans clean. We can educate ourselves about the causes of habitat destruction. We can spread the word to others. Knowledge are a powerful tool in the world of our environment. The sea turtles is counting on us.

　　Sea turtles grow in many sizes and colors. They range between 100 and 1300 pounds. Instead of teeth, sea turtles have beaks in their jaws. Which of their senses is most keen? That would be their sense of smell. A female sea turtle lays her eggs on land. Unfortunately, sea turtles are in danger. But in the last 100 years, the population has become almost extinct. What can we do to ensure the survival of sea turtles? We can all help by keeping our oceans clean. We can educate ourselves about the causes of habitat destruction. We can spread the word to others. Knowledge is a powerful tool in the world of our environment. The sea turtles are counting on us.

Try It
Write a nonfiction paragraph about a reptile or insect that interests you. Underline the subjects of each sentence and circle the verbs.

Answers will vary.

Page 26

Action verbs tell the action of the sentence. Action verbs come in both regular and irregular forms. They have present, past, and future tense forms, too.

Sandy and Karen *visit* every spring.
Sandy and Karen *visited* last year.
Sandy and Karen will *visit* next winter.

I bet Stan and Mike *eat* the whole apple pie.
I *ate* the whole apple.
I will *eat* the apple after I wash it.

Solve It
Look at the following pictures. On the line below each picture, write the action verb that the subject in the picture is doing.

1. _____
2. _____

Answers may vary. Accept all reasonable answers.

3. _____
4. _____

5. _____
6. _____

Page 27

Match It
One verb that is used very often in dialogue is *said*. Try to bring more variety to your writing by using other action verbs as a substitute for the verb *said*. Match the sentences in Column A with an action verb in Column B that could be substituted for the verb *said* in the sentence.

Column A

1. "Hey! We're over here!" said Marty. __c__
2. "I like taking _____, said Kim. __e__

Answers may vary. Possible answers :

3. "_____, said Alex. __i__
4. "_____ want to do more homework," said Justin. __h__
5. "We received 8 inches of snow over night," said the weather person. __d__
6. "Those are the results of my survey," said the professor. __a__
7. "Be careful riding on the wet pavement," said Mom. __g__
8. "Would you like some more lemonade?" said the server. __j__
9. "I don't like what's on my sandwich," said the customer. __f__
10. "Let's start today's lesson," said the teacher. __b__

Column B

a. concluded
b. began
c. yelled
d. reported
e. added
f. complained
g. cautioned
h. groaned
i. vowed
j. asked

Try It
Write a letter to a friend or relative. Tell him or her about a recent event in school or another activity in which you participated. Use at least 10 action verbs. Underline the verbs in your letter.

Answers will vary.

Helping verbs are not main verbs. They help to form some of the tenses of the main verbs. Helping verbs express time and mood.

shall	may	would	has	can
will	have	should	do	did
could	had	must		

The forms of the verb *to be* are also helping verbs:

is	are	was	were	am	been

Verbs ending in **ing** can be a clue that there is a helping verb in the sentence. Sometimes, there is more than one helping verb in a sentence. This is called a **verb phrase**.

The Olympic star *would practice* for hours.
The Olympic star *was practicing* for hours and hours.
The Olympic star *had been practicing* for hours and hours.

Complete It
Choose a helping verb or verb phrase from the box to complete each sentence. Underline the main verb of the sentence that it helps. The main verb does not always directly follow the helping verb. Sometimes there is another word in between. Some sentences can have more than one answer.

have	has	should	must	shall
had	could	would	can	had been

1. _____Shall_____ we <u>dance</u> to this song?
2. That _____could_____ be the right direction, but I m not sure.
3. Rick and Dana _____had been_____ waiting for hours when they finally got in.
4. _____Would_____ you <u>go</u> with me to the movie?
5. The children _____can_____ <u>go</u> with *(Answers may vary. Possible answers :)*
6. I _____have_____ been a fan of hers f...
7. It _____has_____ been days since we ve seen each other.
8. We _____should_____ <u>take</u> this train; it will get us home faster.
9. It _____must_____ <u>be</u> this way, I see a familiar house.
10. This assignment _____has_____ <u>taken</u> a long time to finish.

28

Proof It
Some of the sentences in the paragraph need helping verbs to make them complete. Insert helping verbs when needed.

^ — inserts words

Glacier National Park
Glacier National Park ^*is* located in Montana. Glacier National Park ^*has been* aptly named. Glaciers left from the ice age remain in the park. Grizzly bears ^*are* said to be the mascot of the park. Rangers said that they ^*have* observed the bears almost human-like behavior. The mountain goats of Glacier National Park live high in the mountains. The visitors ^*must* go high up to find them. Glacier National Park ^*is* known as one of the top night spots of the national parks. Because it is located far av... *Answers may vary.* ...llions of stars ^*can be* seen at night. You ^*can* visit Glacier Natio...ark any time of year.

Try It
Write a nonfiction paragraph about a historical place. Use at least ten helping verbs or verb phrases.

Answers will vary.

29

Linking verbs connect a subject to a noun or adjective. They do not express an action.

The most common linking verbs are the forms of the verb *to be*:

is	are	was	were	been	am

Other linking verbs are those of the five senses:

smell	look	taste	feel	sound

Other linking verbs reflect a state of being:

appear	seem	become	grow	remain

A verb or adjective will follow these linking verbs in the sentence.

Identify It
Circle the linking verb and underline the noun or adjective that is linked in each sentence.

1. The crowd (appears) <u>excited</u>.
2. The crowd thought the play (was) <u>good</u>.
3. The lettuce (tastes) <u>bitter</u>.
4. The line (seems) <u>long</u>.
5. Syd, Mitzi, and Deb (were) <u>runners</u>.
6. Mr. Thomas (became) <u>successful</u> after much hard work.
7. The runners (feel) <u>great</u> running in the fresh air.
8. The lights (grew) <u>dim</u> as the play began.
9. The singer s voice (sounds) <u>weak</u> compared to the others.
10. Her future (remains) <u>uncertain</u>.
11. It (has) <u>been</u> a long day.
12. Dinner (sounds) <u>great</u>.
13. They (are) <u>late</u>.
14. I (am) <u>hungry</u>.
15. The snack (is) <u>tasty</u>.

30

Rewrite It
Rewrite the paragraph, replacing the underlined helping verbs with linking verbs. Use the lists of linking verbs on page 30 if you need help.

Don and Tina spent Saturday afternoon at the museum. The paintings <u>were</u> thought-provoking the longer they looked at them. The sculptures <u>were</u> tasteful. The artifacts <u>were</u> fascinating. The rooms <u>were</u> quiet as they walked through each one. They stopped for a snack at the caf . The coffee <u>was</u> wonderful. The muffins <u>were</u> delicious. They stopped at the gift shop before they left the museum. The post cards of some of the paintings <u>were</u> perfect for Don s nieces. Don and Tina enjoyed the afternoon. At the end of the day, they <u>were</u> tired and were ready to go home. However, the museum <u>is</u> one of their favorite places to visit. They <u>are</u> special when they go.

Answers will vary.

Try It
Write a paragraph about a place you like to visit. Give information and details about this place. Use at least five linking verbs in your paragraph.

Answers will vary.

31

Answer Key

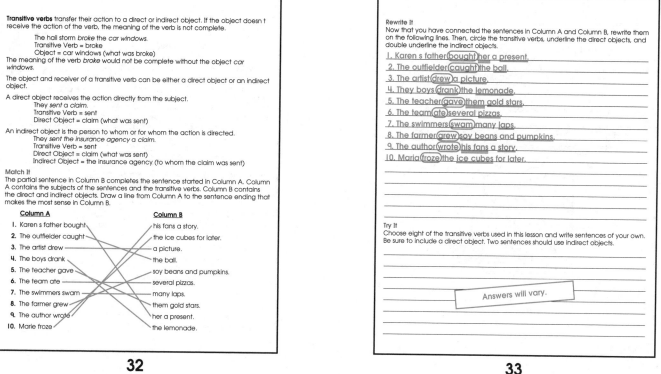

Transitive verbs transfer their action to a direct or indirect object. If the object doesn t receive the action of the verb, the meaning of the verb is not complete.

> The hail storm *broke* the *car windows*.
> Transitive Verb = broke
> Object = car windows (what was broke)

The meaning of the verb *broke* would not be complete without the object *car windows*.

The object and receiver of a transitive verb can be either a direct object or an indirect object.

A direct object receives the action directly from the subject.

> They *sent* a *claim*.
> Transitive Verb = sent
> Direct Object = claim (what was sent)

An indirect object is the person to whom or for whom the action is directed.

> They *sent the insurance agency* a *claim*.
> Transitive Verb = sent
> Direct Object = claim (what was sent)
> Indirect Object = the insurance agency (to whom the claim was sent)

Match It
The partial sentence in Column B completes the sentence started in Column A. Column A contains the subjects of the sentences and the transitive verbs. Column B contains the direct and indirect objects. Draw a line from Column A to the sentence ending that makes the most sense in Column B.

Column A	Column B
1. Karen s father bought	his fans a story.
2. The outfielder caught	the ice cubes for later.
3. The artist drew	a picture.
4. The boys drank	the ball.
5. The teacher gave	soy beans and pumpkins.
6. The team ate	several pizzas.
7. The swimmers swam	many laps.
8. The farmer grew	them gold stars.
9. The author wrote	her a present.
10. Marie froze	the lemonade.

32

Rewrite It
Now that you have connected the sentences in Column A and Column B, rewrite them on the following lines. Then, circle the transitive verbs, underline the direct objects, and double underline the indirect objects.

1. Karen s father (bought) her a present.
2. The outfielder (caught) the ball.
3. The artist (drew) a picture.
4. They boys (drank) the lemonade.
5. The teacher (gave) them gold stars.
6. The team (ate) several pizzas.
7. The swimmers (swam) many laps.
8. The farmer (grew) soy beans and pumpkins.
9. The author (wrote) his fans a story.
10. Maria (froze) the ice cubes for later.

Try It
Choose eight of the transitive verbs used in this lesson and write sentences of your own. Be sure to include a direct object. Two sentences should use indirect objects.

Answers will vary.

33

Gerunds, participles, and **infinitives** are other kinds of verbs. These verbs take the role of another part of speech in some circumstances.

A **gerund** is when a verb is used as a noun. A verb can take the form of the noun when the ending **–ing** is added.

> *Cooking* is one of my favorite activities.
> (The subject *cooking* is a noun in the sentence.)

A **participle** is when a verb is used as an adjective. A verb can take the form of an adjective when the endings **–ing** or **–ed** are added.

> Those *falling* snowflakes from the sky are pretty.
> (*falling* modifies *snowflakes*)
> The *ordered* parts should be here on Monday.
> (*ordered* modifies *parts*)

An **infinitive** is when a verb is used as a noun, adjective, or adverb. A verb can take the form of a noun, adjective, or adverb when preceded by the word *to*.

> *To agree* with the professor can be important.
> (The verb *to agree* acts as the subject, noun, of the sentence.)
> The last student *to report* on the subject led the research team.
> (The verb *to report* acts as an adjective modifying *student*.)
> Roger observed the long movie *to report* on it for the paper.
> (The verb *to report* acts as an adverb modifying *observed*.)

Complete It
Choose a word from the box to fill in the blanks in the sentences.

to catch to drink	joking reported	sleeping to warn

1. _____Sleeping_____ is Jed s favorite activity on the weekends.
2. She jumped high _____to catch_____ the ball.
3. The _____joking_____ comedians performed at school.
4. Jim takes plenty of water _____to drink_____ on long runs.
5. The _____reported_____ details of the event were surprising.
6. _____To warn_____ the public of the oncoming storm was her job.

34

Identify It
The following sentences contain verbs that are acting as gerunds, participles, or infinitives. Identify which by placing a **G** for gerund, a **P** for participle, or an **I** for infinitive after each sentence. Then, underline the gerund, participle, or infinitive.

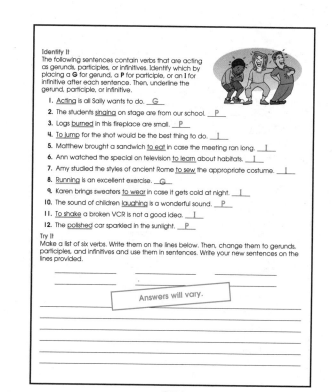

1. Acting is all Sally wants to do. __G__
2. The students singing on stage are from our school. __P__
3. Logs burned in this fireplace are small. __P__
4. To jump for the shot would be the best thing to do. __I__
5. Matthew brought a sandwich to eat in case the meeting ran long. __I__
6. Ann watched the special on television to learn about habitats. __I__
7. Amy studied the styles of ancient Rome to sew the appropriate costume. __I__
8. Running is an excellent exercise. __G__
9. Karen brings sweaters to wear in case it gets cold at night. __I__
10. The sound of children laughing is a wonderful sound. __P__
11. To shake a broken VCR is not a good idea. __I__
12. The polished car sparkled in the sunlight. __P__

Try It
Make a list of six verbs. Write them on the lines below. Then, change them to gerunds, participles, and infinitives and use them in sentences. Write your new sentences on the lines provided.

Answers will vary.

35

Answer Key

Adjectives are words used to describe a noun or pronoun. Most adjectives are common adjectives. Common adjectives are not proper, so they are not capitalized.

The *cold* water felt good on the *hot* day.
Water and *day* are the nouns. The adjectives *cold* and *hot* describe the nouns.

Proper adjectives are formed from proper nouns and are always capitalized.
The children wanted snow cones and *French* fries at the amusement park.
The proper adjective *French* describes the noun, *fries*.

Solve It
The words in the box are adjectives of the senses. Find and circle these words in the puzzle. They can be horizontal, vertical, diagonal, forward, and backward.

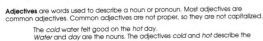

bright	loud	fresh	sour	cool
dim	sharp	sweet	spicy	rough
pretty	soothing	woodsy	tart	soft

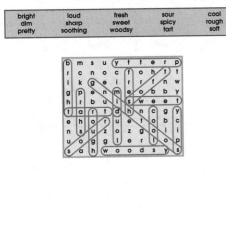

36

Circle the common adjectives and underline the proper adjectives in the paragraph.

Marblehead Lighthouse

Lighthouses are tall towers with bright lights that guide ships at night or in the fog. One famous lighthouse is located in Marblehead, Ohio, on Lake Erie. It is one of Lake Erie's most-photographed landmarks. Marblehead Lighthouse is the oldest lighthouse in continuous operation on the Great Lakes. It has been in operation since 1822. The 65-foot high tower is made of limestone. Throughout the years, the lighthouse has been operated by 15 lighthouse keepers. Two of the 15 keepers were women. Lighthouse keepers had many duties. They lighted the projection lamps, kept logs of passing ships, recorded the weather, and organized rescue efforts. As technology changed with time, the type of light used also changed. Electric light replaced lanterns in 1923. Today a 300mm lens flashes green signals every six seconds. It can be seen for up to 11 nautical miles. The lighthouse no longer has a resident keeper. The United States Coast Guard now operates the Marblehead Lighthouse. The lighthouse beacon continues to warn sailors and keep those on the lake waters safe.

Try It
Choose 10 of the 15 sensory adjectives from the puzzle on page 36. Use each of the 10 adjectives in a sentence.

Answers will vary.

37

Adverbs are words used to modify a verb, an adjective, or another adverb.

An adverb tells *how, why, when, where, how often,* and *how much.*

Adverbs often end in **ly** (but not always).
how or *why:* softly, courageously, forcefully
when or *how often:* sometimes, yesterday, always
where: here, inside, below
how much: generously, barely, liberally

Match It
The categories in Column A are missing their adverbs. Select adverbs from Column B and write them in the appropriate category in Column A.

Column A	Column B
Category 1: how or why	scarcely
cleverly	today
joyfully	cleverly
luckily	outside
	joyfully
Category 2: when or how often	entirely
today	there
tomorrow	tomorrow
never	never
	luckily
Category 3: where	wholly
outside	up
there	
up	
Category 4: how much	
scarcely	
entirely	
wholly	

38

Identify It
Circle the adverbs in the following paragraphs. Underline the verbs, adjectives, or adverbs they modify.

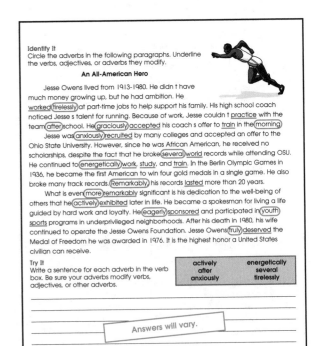

An All-American Hero

Jesse Owens lived from 1913-1980. He didn't have much money growing up, but he had ambition. He worked tirelessly at part-time jobs to help support his family. His high school coach noticed Jesse's talent for running. Because of work, Jesse couldn't practice with the team after school. He graciously accepted his coach's offer to train in the morning.

Jesse was anxiously recruited by many colleges and accepted an offer to the Ohio State University. However, since he was African American, he received no scholarships, despite the fact that he broke several world records while attending OSU. He continued to energetically work, study, and train. In the Berlin Olympic Games in 1936, he became the first American to win four gold medals in a single game. He also broke many track records. Remarkably, his records lasted more than 20 years.

What is even more remarkably significant is his dedication to the well-being of others that he actively exhibited later in life. He became a spokesman for living a life guided by hard work and loyalty. He eagerly sponsored and participated in youth sports programs in underprivileged neighborhoods. After his death in 1980, his wife continued to operate the Jesse Owens Foundation. Jesse Owens truly deserved the Medal of Freedom he was awarded in 1976. It is the highest honor a United States civilian can receive.

Try It
Write a sentence for each adverb in the verb box. Be sure your adverbs modify verbs, adjectives, or other adverbs.

actively	energetically
after	several
anxiously	tirelessly

Answers will vary.

39

Answer Key

Conjunctions connect individual words or groups of words in sentences. There are three types of conjunctions.

Coordinate conjunctions connect words, phrases, or independent clauses that are equal or of the same type. Coordinate conjunctions are *and, but, or, nor, for,* and *yet.*
> The horse s mane is soft *and* shiny.

Correlative conjunctions are used with pairs and are used together. *Both/and, either/or,* and *neither/nor* are examples of correlative conjunctions.
> *Neither* pizza *nor* pasta was listed on the menu.

Subordinate conjunctions connect two clauses that are not equal. They connect dependent clauses to independent clauses in order to complete the meaning. *After, as long as, since,* and *while* are examples of subordinate conjunctions.
> We can t save for our spring vacation *until* we get part time jobs.

Match It
Match the words in Column A with their relationship in Column B.

Column A

1. provided that the light is green
2. cold and fluffy snow
3. either smooth or crunchy

Column B

- equal (coordinate)
- pairs (correlative)
- dependent (subordinate)

4. both mushrooms and olives
5. before it gets dark
6. purple or blue shirt

- equal (coordinate)
- pairs (correlative)
- dependent (subordinate)

7. after the race
8. neither pennies nor nickels
9. music and dance

- equal (coordinate)
- pairs (correlative)
- dependent (subordinate)

40

Identify It
Identify whether the following sentences use coordinate, correlative, or subordinate conjunctions by writing a **CD** for coordinate, **CR** for correlative, or **S** for subordinate before each sentence. Then, underline the conjunctions.

1. __CD__ Bobcats, members of the lynx family, are found in North America <u>and</u> Northern Eurasia.
2. __S__ <u>Although</u> they are members of the lynx family, they differ in a number of ways.
3. __CD__ Bobcats have smaller ear tufts <u>and</u> feet than lynxes.
4. __S__ <u>Because</u> of the terrain bobcats can have different body types.
5. __CD__ Bobcats living in northern territories are smaller <u>and</u> have pale coats.
6. __CD__ Bobcats living in southern territories are larger <u>and</u> have dark coats.
7. __CD__ Bobcats can be found in swampy areas <u>but</u> also desert areas.
8. __CR__ Bobcats hunt <u>both</u> during the night <u>and</u> during the day.
9. __S__ <u>Though</u> smaller in size, bobcats are more aggressive than lynxes.
10. __CD__ Bobcats can climb <u>and</u> swim well.
11. __CR__ <u>Not only</u> bobcats <u>but</u> all big cats are exploited for their fur.
12. __C__ <u>Because</u> of this and other threats to the cat family, conservation groups are working to halt species extinction.

Try It
Write six sentences that use conjunctions. Write two sentences using coordinate conjunctions, two sentences using correlative conjunctions, and two sentences using subordinate conjunctions.

> Answers will vary.

41

An **interjection** is a word or phrase used to express surprise or strong emotion.

Common interjections include: ah; alas; aw; cheers; eeek; eh; hey; hi; huh; hurray; oh; oh, no; ouch; uh; uh-huh; uh-uh; voila; wow; yeah

Exclamation marks are usually used after interjections to separate them from the rest of the sentence.
> Hurray! We are the champions!

If the feeling isn t quite as strong, a comma is used in place of the exclamation point.
> Yeah, the Oakdale Grizzlies had a great basketball season!

Sometimes question marks are used as an interjection s punctuation.
> Well? How does the team look for next year?

Solve It
What interjection from the above list would you choose to add to the following sentences? Use the pictures to help you decide. Write them on the blank in the sentences.

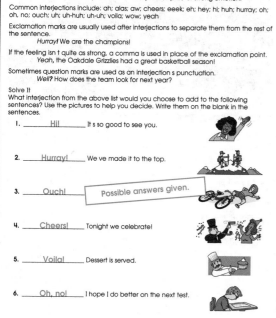

1. ____Hi!____ It s so good to see you.

2. ____Hurray!____ We ve made it to the top.

3. ____Ouch!____   Possible answers given.

4. ____Cheers!____ Tonight we celebrate!

5. ____Voila!____ Dessert is served.

6. ____Oh, no!____ I hope I do better on the next test.

42

Rewrite It
Rewrite the following dialogue. Add interjections where you think they are appropriate to make the dialogue more exciting and interesting. Choose interjections from the previous page, or add some of your own.

We re about ready to land. Look at that landscape, exclaimed Dana as the plane made its descent at the Kona International Airport on the big island, Hawaii. The guide book says this airport sits on miles of lava rock.

How can that be? asked Gabriella.

There are five volcanoes on Hawaii. One is extinct, one is dormant, and three are still active, answered Dana.

There are active volcanoes here? uttered Gabriella.

The one that caused the lava flow beneath this airport is Hualalai, reported Dana. It is still considered active. In the 1700s, it spewed lava all the way to the ocean. The airport is on top of one of the flows. The world s largest volcano, Mauna Loa, and the world s most active volcano, [...] Hawaii.

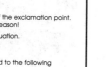
Answers may vary.
Possible answers :

Dana, are you sure y[...]d? asked Gabriella.

I plan to visit all of the [...]

I m hitting the beach. I ve got some serious surfing to do! exclaimed Gabriella.

____Oh, boy! We re about ready to land. Look at that landscape, exclaimed Dana as the plane made its descent at the Kona International Airport on the big island, Hawaii. The guide book says this airport sits on miles of lava rock.

____Eh? How can that be? asked Gabriella.

____Well, there are five volcanoes on Hawaii. One is extinct, one is dormant, and three are still active, answered Dana.

____Oh, my! There are active volcanoes here? uttered Gabriella.

____Yep! The one that caused the lava flow beneath this airport is Hualalai, reported Dana. It is still considered active. In the 1700s, it spewed lava all the way to the ocean. The airport is on top of one of the flows. Eeek! The world s largest volcano, Mauna Loa, and the world s most active volcano, Kilauea, are also here on Hawaii.

____Um, Dana, are you sure you want to vacation on this island? asked Gabriella.

____Oh, yes! I plan to visit all of the volcanoes, answered Dana.

____OK, but I m hitting the beach. I ve got some serious surfing to do! exclaimed Gabriella.

43

Answer Key

Prepositions are words or groups of words that show the relationship between a noun or pronoun (the object of the sentence) and another word in the sentence.
They sat *upon the dock*.
In this sentence, *upon* is the preposition, and *dock* is the object of the preposition.

Common prepositions:

above	below	in	under
across	beneath	inside	until
after	beside	into	up
along	between	near	with
around	by	off	within
at	down	on	without
away	during	outside	
because	except	over	
before	for	to	
behind	from	toward	

Complete It
Complete the following sentences by circling the preposition that works best in the sentence.

1. Look (behind, down from) your car before you back out.
2. I really like the little caf right (across, away from) the street.
3. The kitty likes watching the birds (outside, toward) the window.
4. Our cats only live (around, inside).
5. Edna stored the photographs (through, underneath) her bed.
6. Cedric can t go on the field trip (within, without) his permission slip.
7. The commentators predicted the outcome of the game (before, until) it was over.
8. The snow piled (on top of, over to) the ice.

44

Identify It
Circle the prepositions and underline the objects of the prepositions in the paragraph.

What Is the West Wing?

The West Wing is located (in) the West House. The President (of) the United States has his office (in) the West Wing. It is called the Oval Office. The West Wing houses the executive staff s offices, (in addition to) the President s office. The chief of staff s office is (across from) the Oval Office. The vice president works (beside) the chief of staff. The press secretary and the communication director s offices are (along) the main corridor. The Roosevelt Room (a conference room), the Cabinet Room (the cabinet is a group (of) advisers who are heads (of) government departments), and the President s secretary s office are a little farther (down) the corridor. (Outside) of the press secretary's window is the Rose Garden. The West Colonnade runs (alongside) the Rose Garden. The Press Room is (inside) the West Colonnade. The Press Room sits (on top of) an old swimming pool. The swimming pool is a remnant (of) Franklin D. Roosevelt s administration. That completes the tour (of) the West Wing.

Try It
Write a paragraph describing the rooms in your home. Tell where the rooms are located and what sits outside of some of the windows. Circle the prepositions you used.

Answers will vary.

45

Prepositional phrases include the prepositions and the objects (nouns or pronouns) that follow the prepositions. A prepositional phrase includes the preposition, the object of the preposition, and the modifiers (describes other words) of the object. Prepositional phrases tell about *when* or *where* something is happening.
They sat *upon the dock*.

If the noun in the prepositional phrase above had modifiers, they would also be included in the prepositional phrase.
They sat *upon the wooden dock*.

Match It
Match the beginnings of sentences in Column A with the prepositional phrases that match them best in Column B.

Column A	Column B
1. The clouds are	within the limits.
2. We can leave now	in the sky.
3. Let s have dinner	after the movie.
4. The lake lies far	in her place.
5. When alphabetizing the files, put the As	outside the window.
6. Annie can t baby sit, so Laurie is coming	in front of the Bs.
7. It was raining so hard it was difficult to see	since the babysitter is here.
8. Swimming is permitted if you stay	beyond the forest.

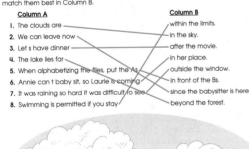

46

Solve It
Possible answers given.

The following sentences _____ the above scene. However, the prepositions are missing. Look at the picture and complete the sentences.

1. The kids played ____inside____ the fence.
2. A cat looked ____through____ a window.
3. A squirrel sat ____on____ the roof.
4. Chimney smoke rose ____above____ the house.
5. The basement was ____below____ the house.
6. The clouds floated ____in____ the sky.
7. The tree sat ____outside____ the fence.
8. A jogger ran ____down____ the street.

Try It
Write four sentences that include prepositional phrases. Underline the prepositional phrases in your sentences.

Answers will vary.

47

Page 48

Articles are specific words that serve as adjectives before a noun. *A*, *an*, and *the* are articles.

The is a **definite article**. That means it names a specific noun.
> I go to *the* school on *the* corner.

The article *the* tells that the person goes to a specific school on a specific corner.

A and *an* are **indefinite articles**. They do not name a specific noun.
> I would like to go to *a* school on *a* corner.

The article *a* tells that the person wants to go to a school on a corner, but not a specific school or corner.

Use *a* when the noun it precedes begins with a consonant or a vowel that sounds like a consonant.
> a dog   a cat   a skunk   a one-way street

Use *an* when the noun it precedes begins with a vowel or sounds like it starts with a vowel.
> an envelope   an olive   an island   an honest person

Complete It
Complete the following sentences by circling the correct answer in parentheses.

1. Mike and Jen rented the apartment above (a, an, (the)) bookstore.
2. Henry wants to get ((a), an, the) car with four doors.
3. An amoeba is ((a), an, the) one-celled animal.
4. Coordinating the play turned out to be quite (a, (an), the) ordeal.
5. Todd wants to rent ((a), an, the) canoe for the weekend.
6. Kay brought (a, (an), the) orange to go with her lunch.
7. (A, An, (The)) orange sweater looked best on Karley.
8. Not (a, (an), the) hour went by that they didn't think about each other.
9. (A, An, (The)) Kensington Trail is beautiful.
10. Lynn wants to buy ((a), an, the) blue or red bracelet.

48

Page 49

Proof It
Proofread the following paragraph. Change any incorrect articles to the correct ones.

> ⟋ — deletes incorrect letters, words, punctuation
> ^ — inserts correct letters, words, punctuation

The Tonys

Almost everyone has heard of the Oscars, an̷ the
Emmys, and a̷ the Golden Globe Awards. The Tony Awards is also a̷ an awards presentation. A̷ The
Tony Awards are given for outstanding accomplishment in theater. The Tony Awards
were named after Antoinette Perry, a̷ an actress, director, producer, and manager. She
was known for helping young people who were interested in the acting profession. A̷ The
first Tony Awards were presented in 1947 with seven categories. Today, there are 25
categories including Best Play and Best Musical. The Tony award is the̷ a medallion that
shows a̷ an image of Antoinette Perry on one side. On a̷ the other side are a̷ the masks of
comedy and tragedy.

Try It
What is your favorite play, movie, or television show? Write a paragraph describing your favorite. Underline the articles you used.

_____
_____
_____
_____

Answers will vary.

_____
_____
_____
_____

49

Page 50

Review: Common and Proper Nouns; Regular Plural Nouns; Irregular Plural Nouns; Personal Pronouns; Demonstrative Pronouns; Relative Pronouns; Indefinite Pronouns

Putting It Together
Complete the following sentences by circling the best answer in parentheses.

1. I like to visit the ((museum), Museum) on Sundays.
2. The New York (museum, (Museum)) of Art is one famous museum.
3. Paul Klee was a famous artist who loved and painted many ((cats), cat).
4. ((Women), Womans) were the subject of many of the paintings of Henri Matisse.
5. Claude Monet's parents did not want (he, (him)) to become an artist.
6. But ((that), those) didn't stop him.
7. Marc Chagall liked to paint violins in memory of his uncle (which, (who)) played.
8. The impressionist artist Pierre-Auguste Renoir believed (anyone, (everyone)) should work with their hands.

Review: Verbs: Regular Present and Past Tense; Verbs: Irregular Present and Past Tense; Subject-Verb Agreement; Action Verbs; Helping Verbs; Linking Verbs; Transitive Verbs; Gerunds, Participles, Infinitives

Circle the regular past tense verb and underline the irregular past tense verb.

1. Last weekend we (played) ball and we built sand castles.

Circle the action verb and underline the helping verb phrase.

2. The golfer (hit) the ball to the left; he should have hit it straight ahead.

Circle the transitive verb and underline its object.

3. The artists (drew) many paintings.

Circle the infinitive.

4. The author is going (to write) at the beach.

50

Page 51

Review: Adjectives; Adverbs; Conjunctions; Interjections; Prepositions; Prepositional Phrases; Articles

Identify adjectives (**ADJ**), adverbs (**ADV**), conjunctions (**C**), prepositions (**P**), and articles (**A**) in the following biography. Write the abbreviation on the line next to the word.

Leonardo da Vinci

One of ___P___ the greatest ___ADJ___ artists of all time was more than just an
___A___ artist. He was a sculptor, scientist, inventor, engineer, astronomer, architect,
musician, philosopher, and ___C___ mathematician. Leonardo da Vinci (1452—1519)
was born in ___P___ Vinci, Italy. Da Vinci was a ___A___ genius. During his lifetime,
he sketched objects that were ahead of ___P___ his time: the ___A___ airplane,
the tank, and ___C___ the submarine. Da Vinci brilliantly ___ADV___ and beautifully
___ADV___ painted the human ___ADJ___ body and other natural ___ADJ___ objects.
He was also a humanitarian.

Born during ___P___ the Renaissance, the ___A___ period in history that
represented the great ___ADJ___ rebirth of art, literature, and learning in 14th, 15th, and
16th century Europe, da Vinci became known as the perfect ___ADJ___ example of
___P___ the Renaissance ___ADJ___ Man. Leonardo da Vinci painted the famous
___ADJ___ *Mona Lisa* and ___C___ *The Last Supper*, both of which now hang in
___P___ The Louvre in Paris, France.

51

Answer Key

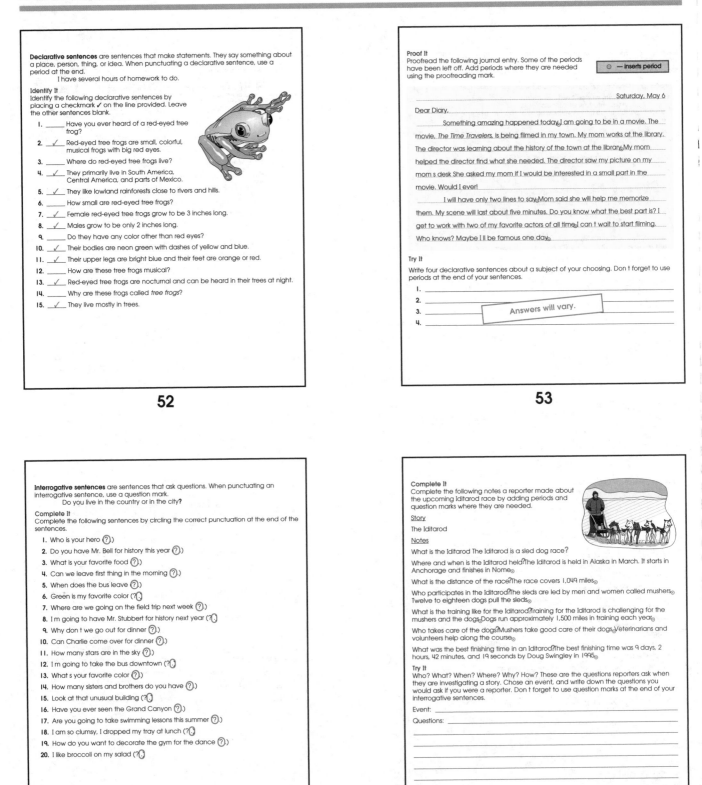

Declarative sentences are sentences that make statements. They say something about a place, person, thing, or idea. When punctuating a declarative sentence, use a period at the end.

    I have several hours of homework to do.

Identify It
Identify the following declarative sentences by placing a checkmark ✓ on the line provided. Leave the other sentences blank.

1. _____ Have you ever heard of a red-eyed tree frog?
2. _✓_ Red-eyed tree frogs are small, colorful, musical frogs with big red eyes.
3. _____ Where do red-eyed tree frogs live?
4. _✓_ They primarily live in South America, Central America, and parts of Mexico.
5. _✓_ They like lowland rainforests close to rivers and hills.
6. _____ How small are red-eyed tree frogs?
7. _✓_ Female red-eyed tree frogs grow to be 3 inches long.
8. _✓_ Males grow to be only 2 inches long.
9. _____ Do they have any color other than red eyes?
10. _✓_ Their bodies are neon green with dashes of yellow and blue.
11. _✓_ Their upper legs are bright blue and their feet are orange or red.
12. _____ How are these tree frogs musical?
13. _✓_ Red-eyed tree frogs are nocturnal and can be heard in their trees at night.
14. _____ Why are these frogs called *tree frogs*?
15. _✓_ They live mostly in trees.

52

Proof It
Proofread the following journal entry. Some of the periods have been left off. Add periods where they are needed using the proofreading mark.

> ⊙ — inserts period

                               Saturday, May 6

Dear Diary,

        Something amazing happened today⊙ I am going to be in a movie. The movie, *The Time Travelers*, is being filmed in my town. My mom works at the library. The director was learning about the history of the town at the library⊙ My mom helped the director find what she needed. The director saw my picture on my mom s desk⊙ She asked my mom if I would be interested in a small part in the movie. Would I ever!

        I will have only two lines to say⊙ Mom said she will help me memorize them. My scene will last about five minutes. Do you know what the best part is? I get to work with two of my favorite actors of all time⊙ I can t wait to start filming. Who knows? Maybe I ll be famous one day⊙

Try It
Write four declarative sentences about a subject of your choosing. Don t forget to use periods at the end of your sentences.

1. _____
2. _____
3. _____ Answers will vary.
4. _____

53

Interrogative sentences are sentences that ask questions. When punctuating an interrogative sentence, use a question mark.

    Do you live in the country or in the city?

Complete It
Complete the following sentences by circling the correct punctuation at the end of the sentences.

1. Who is your hero ⑦.)
2. Do you have Mr. Bell for history this year ⑦.)
3. What is your favorite food ⑦.)
4. Can we leave first thing in the morning ⑦.)
5. When does the bus leave ⑦.)
6. Green is my favorite color (?⊙)
7. Where are we going on the field trip next week ⑦.)
8. I m going to have Mr. Stubbert for history next year (?⊙)
9. Why don t we go out for dinner ⑦.)
10. Can Charlie come over for dinner ⑦.)
11. How many stars are in the sky ⑦.)
12. I m going to take the bus downtown (?⊙)
13. What s your favorite color ⑦.)
14. How many sisters and brothers do you have ⑦.)
15. Look at that unusual building (?⊙)
16. Have you ever seen the Grand Canyon ⑦.)
17. Are you going to take swimming lessons this summer ⑦.)
18. I am so clumsy, I dropped my tray at lunch (?⊙)
19. How do you want to decorate the gym for the dance ⑦.)
20. I like broccoli on my salad (?⊙)

54

Complete It
Complete the following notes a reporter made about the upcoming Iditarod race by adding periods and question marks where they are needed.

Story

The Iditarod

Notes

What is the Iditarod⊙ The Iditarod is a sled dog race?

Where and when is the Iditarod held⊙ The Iditarod is held in Alaska in March. It starts in Anchorage and finishes in Nome⊙

What is the distance of the race⊙ The race covers 1,049 miles⊙

Who participates in the Iditarod⊙ The sleds are led by men and women called mushers⊙ Twelve to eighteen dogs pull the sleds⊙

What is the training like for the Iditarod⊙ Training for the Iditarod is challenging for the mushers and the dogs⊙ Dogs run approximately 1,500 miles in training each year⊙

Who takes care of the dogs⊙ Mushers take good care of their dogs⊙ Veterinarians and volunteers help along the course⊙

What was the best finishing time in an Iditarod⊙ The best finishing time was 9 days, 2 hours, 42 minutes, and 19 seconds by Doug Swingley in 1995⊙

Try It
Who? What? When? Where? Why? How? These are the questions reporters ask when they are investigating a story. Chose an event, and write down the questions you would ask if you were a reporter. Don t forget to use question marks at the end of your interrogative sentences.

Event: _____

Questions: _____

_____

_____

_____

_____

_____

55

Exclamatory sentences are sentences that reveal urgency, strong surprise, or emotion. When punctuating an exclamatory sentence, use an exclamation mark.
     Watch out for the icy steps!

Sometimes you will find interjections in exclamatory sentences.
     Yea! One more test until summer break!

Exclamation marks can also be used in dialogue, when the character or speaker is making an urgent or emotional statement.
     Watch out! shouted Kelly.

Exclamation marks should be used sparingly in writing. Do not overuse them.

Match It
Match the sentences (which are missing their punctuation) in Column A with their type of sentence in Column B. Draw an arrow to make your match.

Column A	Column B
1. I will be thirteen on my next birthday	declarative
2. Hurry and open up your presents	interrogative
3. How old are you	exclamatory

4. Oh no I dropped all of my papers in a puddle	declarative
5. Is it supposed to snow all weekend	interrogative
6. Autumn is my favorite season	exclamatory

7. Where are my shoes	declarative
8. I scored 12 points in the basketball game	interrogative
9. Look out	exclamatory

56

Proof It
Proofread the following skit. Add periods, question marks, or exclamation marks on the spaces.

     Karen and Dave, shouted Sandra, we re going to a planetarium !

     What is a planetarium ? questioned Karen.

     A planetarium, answered Sandra, is a room with a large dome ceiling . Images of the sky are projected onto the ceiling with a star projector.

     Dave continued, You can see the movements of the sun, moon, planets, and stars . I ve always wanted to go to a planetarium !

     Sandra said, They shorten the time so you can see in just minutes what it takes the objects years to complete .

     Will we be able to see the constellations of the zodiac ? asked Karen.

     Yes, I believe so, answered Dave. We will even be able to see how the objects in the sky will look thousands of years from now !

     We ll sit in seats like we re at the movie theater, but it will really look like we re outside, said Sandra.

     Karen exclaimed, I can t wait to go to the planetarium !

Try It
Write four sentence pairs. Write four declarative sentences using periods as the end punctuation. Then, write four similar sentences that show stronger emotion or surprise. You can add interjections if you like. Be sure to change the end punctuation to an exclamation mark.

Declarative Sentences
1. _____
2. _____
3. _____
4. _____

Exclamatory Sentences
1. _____   *Answers will vary.*
2. _____
3. _____
4. _____

57

Imperative sentences demand that an action be performed. The subjects of imperative sentences are usually not expressed. They usually contain the understood subject *you*. Imperative sentences can be punctuated with a period or an exclamation mark.
     Get on bus #610.
     (*You* get on bus #610.)

     Answer the phone before it stops ringing!
     (*You* answer the phone before it stops ringing!)

Identify It
Identify the following sentences by writing a **D** for declarative, an **IN** for interrogative, and **E** for exclamatory, or an **IM** for imperative after each sentence.

1. Hop over that puddle! __IM__
2. How many more days until spring break? __IN__
3. I won the contest! __E__
4. I don t want anchovies on my pizza. __D__
5. Let s set up a lemonade stand this summer. __D__
6. What is the distance of a century bicycle ride? __IN__
7. Announce the winners as they come across the finish line. __D__
8. The firefighter saved everyone in the house! __E__
9. Think about what you want to serve at the party. __IM__
10. My favorite appetizer is vegetable stuffed mushrooms. __D__
11. Whom do you admire most? __IN__
12. The fundraiser was a huge success! __E__

58

Complete It
Use periods, question marks, and exclamation marks to complete the sentences.

1. What are the largest trees in the world?
2. Redwood trees are the largest trees in the world.
3. Redwoods can grow to be 240 feet tall !
4. How long do redwoods live?
5. Redwoods can live more than 2000 years !
6. Where can I find redwood trees?
7. Redwood trees are located along the Pacific Coast in the United States.
8. Redwood fossils have been found all over the world .
9. Fossils from redwood trees have been found from as long ago as 160 million years !
10. Wow! I want to see the redwood trees !

Possible answers given.

Try It
Write a dialogue with four characters. Two of the characters have just won something at a school raffle. The other characters are waiting to hear if their raffle number is called. In your skit, use declarative, interrogative, exclamatory, and imperative sentences.

_____
_____
_____
_____
_____
     Answers will vary.
_____
_____
_____
_____
_____

59

Simple sentences are sentences with one independent clause. **Independent clauses** present a complete thought and can stand alone as a sentence. Simple sentences do not have any dependent clauses. **Dependent clauses** do not present a complete thought and cannot stand alone as sentences.

Simple sentences can have one or more subjects.
    Goats lived at the sanctuary.
    Goats and *turkeys* lived at the sanctuary.

Simple sentences can have one or more predicates.
    The goats *played* with the other animals.
    The turkeys *played* and *talked* with the other animals.

Simple sentences can have more than one subject and more than one predicate.
    The *goats* and the *turkeys played* and *talked* with the other animals.

Match It
Each of the simple sentences in Column A has select words underlined. The parts of speech that match the underlined words are found in Column B. Match the sentences in Column A with the parts of speech in Column B.

Column A

1. Farm Sanctuary <u>rescues</u> and <u>protects</u> farm animals.

2. <u>Farm Sanctuary members</u> have helped to pass farm animal protection laws.

3. The <u>New York sanctuary</u> and the <u>California sanctuary</u> are home to hundreds of rescued farm animals.

4. Farm Sanctuary <u>offers</u> a humane education program to schools.

5. At Farm Sanctuary, <u>people</u> and <u>animals</u> <u>work</u> and <u>play</u> together.

Column B

one subject

two subjects

one predicate

two predicates

two subjects/two predicates

60

Identify It
Identify the subjects and predicates in the following simple sentences from a paragraph from a travel brochure. Circle the subject and underline the predicate of each sentence.

Hike, Bike, See Amazing Wildlife

(You) can experience the great outdoors at Acadia National Park in Maine. (Many visitors) hike and bike the miles of trails. (Some trails) have moderate to difficult climbs. (More than 225 types of birds) live in Acadia. (Songbirds) are popular in the spring. (The winter) brings the chickadees. (Eagles, peregrine falcons, and ospreys) inhabit Acadia. Perhaps (the most famous birds) are the Atlantic Puffins. (Maine) is the only place in the United States where puffins breed. (Visitors) who canoe and kayak can see puffins from the nearby bay. (You) can also take a specifically designed Puffin Cruise. (You) shouldn t miss the beauty of America s first national park east of the Mississippi.

Try It
Write the simple sentences as noted below.

1. one subject

2. more than one subject

3. one predicate

Answers will vary.

4. more than one predicate

5. more than one subject and more than one predicate

61

Compound sentences are sentences with two or more simple sentences (independent clauses) joined by a coordinate conjunction, punctuation, or both. As in simple sentences, there are no dependent clauses in compound sentences.

A compound sentence can be two sentences joined with a comma and a coordinate conjunction.
    He didn t think he was a fan of Shakespeare, *yet* he enjoyed the play.

A compound sentence can also be two simple sentences joined by a semicolon.
    He didn t think he was a fan of Shakespeare; he enjoyed the play.

Match It
Match simple sentences in Column A with simple sentences in Column B to create compound sentences. Write the compound sentences and remember to add either a coordinate conjunction or punctuation.

Column A

1. The football game was exciting.

2. My favorite team is playing.

3. My school s colors are blue and white.

4. I m going to get a [pretzel at halftime].

5. My team won the [game].

Column B

1. They have a good record this year.

2. I m going to get pizza after the game.

3. The score as close.

4. ...n t over yet.

5. The opposing team s colors are green and gold.

Answers will vary.

1. The football game was exciting; the score was close.

2. My favorite team is playing, and they have a good record this year.

3. My school s colors are blue and white; the opposing team s colors are green and gold.

4. I m going to get a pretzel at halftime, or I m going to get pizza after the game.

5. My team won the game, but the season isn t over yet.

62

Rewrite It
Rewrite the following paragraph, changing simple sentences to compound sentences. Combine the sentences with coordinate conjunctions or semicolons.

What is a triathlon?

A triathlon is a unique sporting event. Three different sports are involved. Participants in a triathlon swim, bike, and run. It is a challenging event. The very first triathlon was held in France in 1921. The name of the event was Course Des Trois Sports (The Race of Three Sports). The first American triathlon was in 1974. It took place in San Diego, California. Hundreds of athletes now participate in triathlons. There s a distance for everyone. The shortest distance is the sprint distance. It consists of a 400-1000 yard swim, an 8-20 mile bike ride, and a 2-5 mile run. The international distance is also the Olympic distance. It has a 1 mile swim, a 24.8 mile bike ride, and a 6.2 mile run. The Ironman is the king of triathlons. It consists of a 2.4 mile swim, a 112 mile bike ride, and a 26.2 mile run. Triathlons are quite challenging. It is not enough. Of course we are always pushing ourselves harder and harder. Now athletes take part in ultratriathlons. What will be next?

Answers will vary.

63

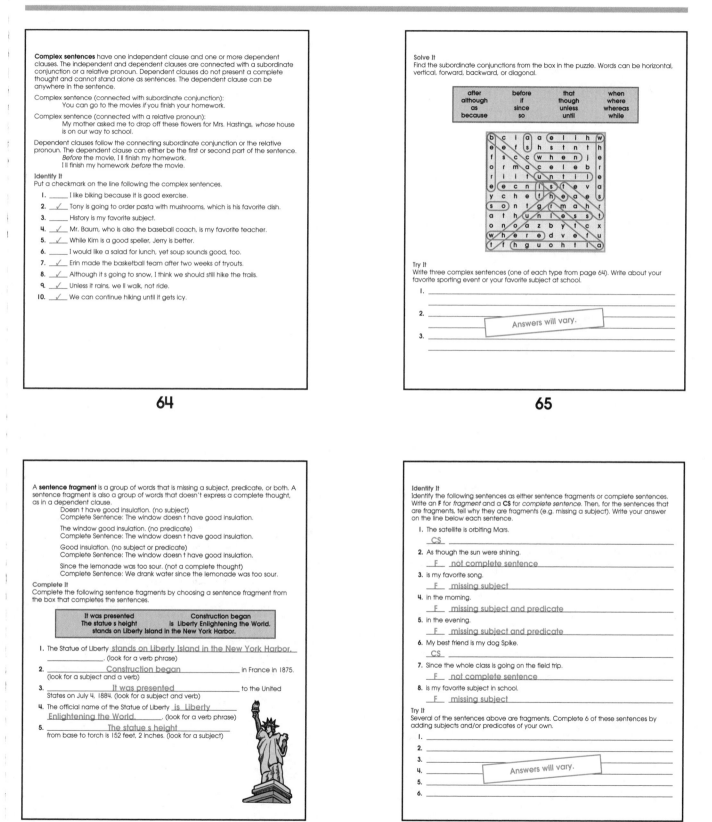

Complex sentences have one independent clause and one or more dependent clauses. The independent and dependent clauses are connected with a subordinate conjunction or a relative pronoun. Dependent clauses do not present a complete thought and cannot stand alone as sentences. The dependent clause can be anywhere in the sentence.

Complex sentence (connected with subordinate conjunction):
    You can go to the movies *if* you finish your homework.

Complex sentence (connected with a relative pronoun):
    My mother asked me to drop off these flowers for Mrs. Hastings, *whose* house is on our way to school.

Dependent clauses follow the connecting subordinate conjunction or the relative pronoun. The dependent clause can either be the first or second part of the sentence.
    Before the movie, I ll finish my homework.
    I ll finish my homework *before* the movie.

Identify It
Put a checkmark on the line following the complex sentences.

1. _____ I like biking because it is good exercise.
2. _✓_ Tony is going to order pasta with mushrooms, which is his favorite dish.
3. _____ History is my favorite subject.
4. _✓_ Mr. Baum, who is also the baseball coach, is my favorite teacher.
5. _✓_ While Kim is a good speller, Jerry is better.
6. _____ I would like a salad for lunch, yet soup sounds good, too.
7. _✓_ Erin made the basketball team after two weeks of tryouts.
8. _✓_ Although it s going to snow, I think we should still hike the trails.
9. _✓_ Unless it rains, we ll walk, not ride.
10. _✓_ We can continue hiking until it gets icy.

64

Solve It
Find the subordinate conjunctions from the box in the puzzle. Words can be horizontal, vertical, forward, backward, or diagonal.

after	before	that	when
although	if	though	where
as	since	unless	whereas
because	so	until	while

Try It
Write three complex sentences (one of each type from page 64). Write about your favorite sporting event or your favorite subject at school.

1. _____
2. _____
    Answers will vary.
3. _____
    _____

65

A **sentence fragment** is a group of words that is missing a subject, predicate, or both. A sentence fragment is also a group of words that doesn't express a complete thought, as in a dependent clause.
    Doesn t have good insulation. (no subject)
    Complete Sentence: The window doesn t have good insulation.

    The window good insulation. (no predicate)
    Complete Sentence: The window doesn t have good insulation.

    Good insulation. (no subject or predicate)
    Complete Sentence: The window doesn t have good insulation.

    Since the lemonade was too sour. (not a complete thought)
    Complete Sentence: We drank water since the lemonade was too sour.

Complete It
Complete the following sentence fragments by choosing a sentence fragment from the box that completes the sentences.

It was presented	Construction began
The statue s height	is Liberty Enlightening the World.
stands on Liberty Island in the New York Harbor.	

1. The Statue of Liberty **stands on Liberty Island in the New York Harbor.**
    _____. (look for a verb phrase)
2. **Construction began** in France in 1875.
    (look for a subject and a verb)
3. **It was presented** to the United
    States on July 4, 1884. (look for a subject and verb)
4. The official name of the Statue of Liberty **is Liberty**
    Enlightening the World. (look for a verb phrase)
5. **The statue s height**
    from base to torch is 152 feet, 2 inches. (look for a subject)

66

Identify It
Identify the following sentences as either sentence fragments or complete sentences. Write an **F** for *fragment* and a **CS** for *complete sentence*. Then, for the sentences that are fragments, tell why they are fragments (e.g. missing a subject). Write your answer on the line below each sentence.

1. The satellite is orbiting Mars.
    _CS_
2. As though the sun were shining.
    _F_ _not complete sentence_
3. is my favorite song.
    _F_ _missing subject_
4. in the morning.
    _F_ _missing subject and predicate_
5. in the evening.
    _F_ _missing subject and predicate_
6. My best friend is my dog Spike.
    _CS_
7. Since the whole class is going on the field trip.
    _F_ _not complete sentence_
8. is my favorite subject in school.
    _F_ _missing subject_

Try It
Several of the sentences above are fragments. Complete 6 of these sentences by adding subjects and/or predicates of your own.

1. _____
2. _____
3. _____
4. _____   Answers will vary.
5. _____
6. _____

67

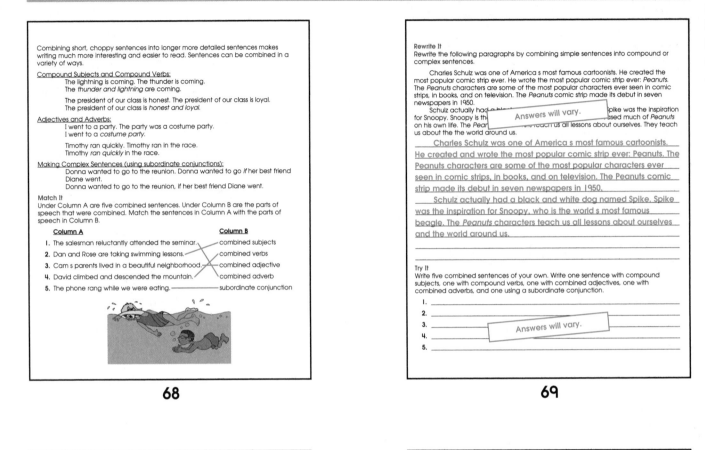

Page 68

Combining short, choppy sentences into longer more detailed sentences makes writing much more interesting and easier to read. Sentences can be combined in a variety of ways.

Compound Subjects and Compound Verbs:
The lightning is coming. The thunder is coming.
The *thunder and lightning* are coming.

The president of our class is honest. The president of our class is loyal.
The president of our class is *honest and loyal.*

Adjectives and Adverbs:
I went to a party. The party was a costume party.
I went to a *costume party.*

Timothy ran quickly. Timothy ran in the race.
Timothy *ran quickly* in the race.

Making Complex Sentences (using subordinate conjunctions):
Donna wanted to go to the reunion. Donna wanted to go *if* her best friend Diane went.
Donna wanted to go to the reunion, if her best friend Diane went.

Match It
Under Column A are five combined sentences. Under Column B are the parts of speech that were combined. Match the sentences in Column A with the parts of speech in Column B.

Column A	Column B
1. The salesman reluctantly attended the seminar.	combined subjects
2. Dan and Rose are taking swimming lessons.	combined verbs
3. Cam s parents lived in a beautiful neighborhood.	combined adjective
4. David climbed and descended the mountain.	combined adverb
5. The phone rang while we were eating.	subordinate conjunction

Page 69

Rewrite It
Rewrite the following paragraphs by combining simple sentences into compound or complex sentences.

Charles Schulz was one of America s most famous cartoonists. He created the most popular comic strip ever. He wrote the most popular comic strip ever: *Peanuts.* The *Peanuts* characters are some of the most popular characters ever seen in comic strips, in books, and on television. The *Peanuts* comic strip made its debut in seven newspapers in 1950.
Schulz actually had a black [Answers will vary.] pike was the inspiration for Snoopy. Snoopy is th[...] on his own life. The *Pear*[...] us all lessons about ourselves. They teach us about the the world around us.

Answers will vary.

Charles Schulz was one of America s most famous cartoonists. He created and wrote the most popular comic strip ever: Peanuts. The Peanuts characters are some of the most popular characters ever seen in comic strips, in books, and on television. The Peanuts comic strip made its debut in seven newspapers in 1950.

Schulz actually had a black and white dog named Spike. Spike was the inspiration for Snoopy, who is the world s most famous beagle. The Peanuts characters teach us all lessons about ourselves and the world around us.

Try It
Write five combined sentences of your own. Write one sentence with compound subjects, one with compound verbs, one with combined adjectives, one with combined adverbs, and one using a subordinate conjunction.

1.
2.
3. Answers will vary.
4.
5.

Page 71

Rewrite It
The sentences in the following paragraph are out of order. Rewrite the paragraph placing the topic sentence first, the summary sentence last, and the body sentences in between.

This substance has a red pigment. Horseshoe crabs blood has copper in it. Not all living creatures have red blood; horseshoe crabs blood is blue! Human blood has hemoglobin that has iron in it. The color of one s blood, whether a creature big or small, depends on the makeup and chemicals in the blood. This material causes the blood to appear blue.

topic sentence: Not all living creatures have red blood; horseshoe crabs blood is blue!

first body sentence: Horseshoe crabs blood has copper in it.

second body sentence: This material causes the blood to appear blue.

third body sentence: Human blood has hemoglobin that has iron in it.

fourth body sentence: This substance has a red pigment.

end sentence: The color of one s blood, whether a creature big or small, depends on the makeup and chemicals in the blood.

Try It
Write a paragraph about a topic of your choosing. Select one of the types of paragraphs. Think about your topic ideas and the five steps of writing.

Answers will vary.

Page 72

Review: Declarative Sentences, Interrogative Sentences, Exclamatory Sentences, Imperative Sentences

Putting It Together
Rewrite the exclamatory sentence as an imperative sentence.
1. You should drink the hot tea slowly!
   Drink the hot tea slowly!

Rewrite the interrogative sentence as a declarative sentence.
2. Are you going to the game on Saturday?
   I m going to the game on Saturday.

Rewrite the imperative sentence as an interrogative sentence.
3. Hit the ball far!
   Did you hit the ball far?

Rewrite the declarative sentence as an imperative sentence.
4. You should recycle the papers instead of putting them in the trash.
   Recycle the papers instead of putting them in the trash.

Review: Simple Sentences, Compound Sentences, Complex Sentences, Sentence Fragments, Combining Sentences

Write whether the following sentences are simple, compound, complex, or a sentence fragment. If they are simple sentences or sentence fragments, rewrite them.
1. She jogged through the mist. She jogged slowly.
   simple; It is a beautiful, inspirational painting.
2. The chefs cooked and baked in the competition.
   compound; no rewrite needed.
3. After dinner, I m going for a walk.
   complex; no rewrite needed.
4. Although I studied hard,
   sentence fragment (rewrites will vary)

Review: Writing a Paragraph

1. What is one of the most important things to do when writing a paragraph?
   Choosing a topic and writing a topic sentence.

2. If you were asked to write a paragraph about your favorite animal, what type of paragraph would that be?
   The paragraph would be an expository paragraph.

3. What do you write in the last sentence of a paragraph?
   The last sentence is a summary of the entire paragraph.

4. If you were asked to write a paragraph that tries to convince your readers of something, what type of paragraph would that be?
   The paragraph would be a persuasive paragraph.

5. What is the body of a paragraph?
   The body of the paragraph gives the information and details that explain the topic sentence.

Now, write a short paragraph about your favorite movie. Remember to use the different parts of a paragraph.

Answers will vary.

73

Proper nouns are specific people, places, and things. They are capitalized.

Capitalize days of the week.
   Sunday Monday Tuesday Wednesday Thursday Friday Saturday

Capitalize months of the year.
   January February March April May June July August September October November December

Months of the year are also capitalized when they serve as adjectives.
   They ran the marathon on a sunny *June* morning.

Solve It
Complete the following sentences by cracking the code and filling in the blanks. Remember to capitalize the days of the weeks when you write them.

1=A	4=D	7=G	10=J	13=M	16=P	19=S	22=V	25=Y
2=B	5=E	8=H	11=K	14=N	17=Q	20=T	23=W	26=Z
3=C	6=F	9=I	12=L	15=O	18=R	21=U	24=X	

1. I'm always groggy on a M o n d a y, the first day of the school week.
   13 15 14 4 1 25

2. I was born on a S u n d a y, one of the two weekend days.
   19 21 14 4 1 25

3. The day of the week with the most letters in it is W e d n e s d a y.
   23 5 14 5 19 4 1 25

4. F r i d a y is high school football night.
   6 18 9 4 1 25

5. T u e s d a y is one of the two days of the week that starts with the
   20 21 5 19 4 1 25   same letter.

6. T h u r s d a y is the other.
   20 8 21 18 19 4 1 25

7. I play baseball every S a t u r d a y.
   19 1 20 21 18 4 1 25

74

Rewrite It
Rewrite the following sentences after unscrambling the names of the months. Do not forget to capitalize them.

1. The month of *jeun* is Adopt a Shelter Cat Month.
   The month of June is Adopt a Shelter Cat Month.

2. Earth Day, a day for environmental awareness, is celebrated in *lpari*.
   Earth Day, a day for environmental awareness, is celebrated in April.

3. Adopt a Shelter Dog Month is held in *cbotore*.
   Adopt a Shelter Dog Month is held in October.

4. St. Valentine is credited for bringing couples together on the 14th of *barufrey*.
   St. Valentine is credited for bringing couples together on the 14th of February.

5. The state of Colorado has its own day, and it s celebrated in *stuagu*.
   The state of Colorado has its own day, and it s celebrated in August.

6. Shogatsu is the name for New Year in Japan; it is celebrated in *najruay*.
   Shogatsu is the name for New Year in Japan; it is celebrated in January.

Try It
Write a paragraph about your favorite day of the week or month of the year.

Answers will vary.

75

Historical events, nationalities, and team names are **proper nouns**, as well.

Events, periods of time, and important documents from history are capitalized.
   Cold War   Renaissance Period   Constitution of the United States

Names of languages and nationalities are capitalized. They are also capitalized when they are used as adjectives.
   French   Hispanic   Dutch apple pie

The names of sports teams are capitalized.
   Detroit Tigers

Complete It
Complete the following sentences by circling the correct answer in parentheses. Hint: not all choices are proper and need to be capitalized.

1. The war lasting from 1939 to 1945 was (world war II, (World War II)).
2. The (italian, (Italian)) language is one of the romance languages.
3. An ((era), Era) is considered to be any important period of time.
4. The season begins for ((baseball teams,) Baseball Teams) in April.
5. Mikhail Baryshnikov is of (russian, (Russian)) descent.
6. The (boston red sox, (Boston Red Sox)) won the World Series in 2004.
7. The (*magna carta*, (*Magna Carta*)) was written in 1215.
8. The (english, (English)) cocker spaniel was the number one dog in popularity in Britain from the 1930s through the 1950s.
9. The (victorian era, (Victorian Era)) lasted from 1839 to 1901, during the reign of Queen Victoria in England.
10. The (french, (French)) souffli is a dessert served warm.
11. The first ten amendments to the *Constitution of the United States* is the (bill of rights, (Bill of Rights)).
12. The (battle of waterloo, (Battle of Waterloo)) took place in Belgium in 1815.

76

Answer Key

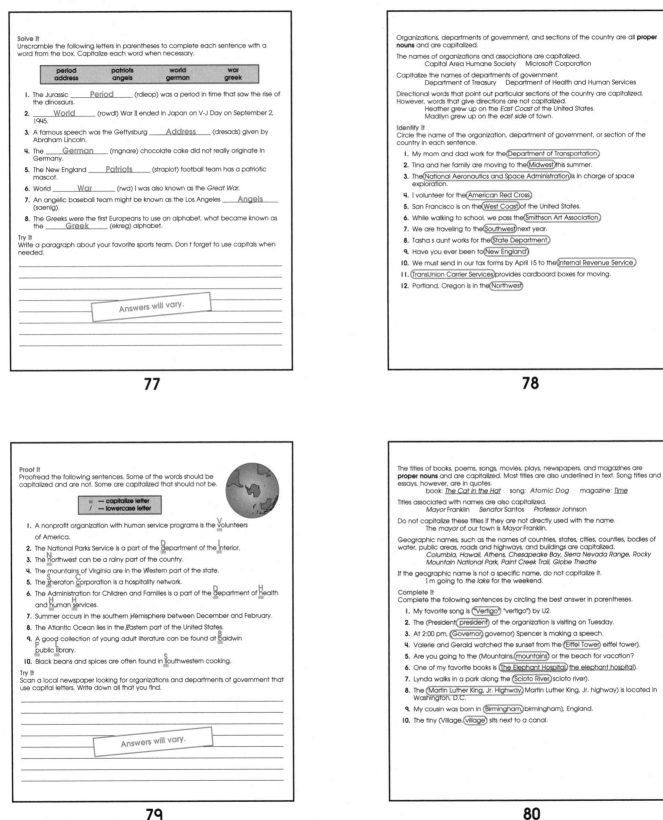

Solve It

Unscramble the following letters in parentheses to complete each sentence with a word from the box. Capitalize each word when necessary.

period	patriots	world	war
address	angels	german	greek

1. The Jurassic ___Period___ (rdieop) was a period in time that saw the rise of the dinosaurs.
2. ___World___ (rowdl) War II ended in Japan on V-J Day on September 2, 1945.
3. A famous speech was the Gettysburg ___Address___ (dresads) given by Abraham Lincoln.
4. The ___German___ (mgnare) chocolate cake did not really originate in Germany.
5. The New England ___Patriots___ (strapiot) football team has a patriotic mascot.
6. World ___War___ (rwa) I was also known as the *Great War*.
7. An angelic baseball team might be known as the Los Angeles ___Angels___ (saenlg).
8. The Greeks were the first Europeans to use an alphabet, what became known as the ___Greek___ (ekreg) alphabet.

Try It

Write a paragraph about your favorite sports team. Don't forget to use capitals when needed.

Answers will vary.

77

Organizations, departments of government, and sections of the country are all **proper nouns** and are capitalized.

The names of organizations and associations are capitalized.
Capital Area Humane Society   Microsoft Corporation

Capitalize the names of departments of government.
Department of Treasury   Department of Health and Human Services

Directional words that point out particular sections of the country are capitalized. However, words that give directions are not capitalized.
Heather grew up on the *East Coast* of the United States.
Madilyn grew up on the *east side* of town.

Identify It

Circle the name of the organization, department of government, or section of the country in each sentence.

1. My mom and dad work for the (Department of Transportation).
2. Tina and her family are moving to the (Midwest) this summer.
3. The (National Aeronautics and Space Administration) is in charge of space exploration.
4. I volunteer for the (American Red Cross).
5. San Francisco is on the (West Coast) of the United States.
6. While walking to school, we pass the (Smithson Art Association).
7. We are traveling to the (Southwest) next year.
8. Tasha's aunt works for the (State Department).
9. Have you ever been to (New England)?
10. We must send in our tax forms by April 15 to the (Internal Revenue Service).
11. (TransUnion Carrier Services) provides cardboard boxes for moving.
12. Portland, Oregon is in the (Northwest).

78

Proof It

Proofread the following sentences. Some of the words should be capitalized and are not. Some are capitalized that should not be.

≡ — capitalize letter
/ — lowercase letter

1. A nonprofit organization with human service programs is the V̲olunteers of America.
2. The National Parks Service is a part of the D̲epartment of the I̲nterior.
3. The N̲orthwest can be a rainy part of the country.
4. The mountains of Virginia are in the W̲estern part of the state.
5. The S̲heraton C̲orporation is a hospitality network.
6. The Administration for Children and Families is a part of the d̲epartment of h̲ealth and h̲uman services.
7. Summer occurs in the southern H̲emisphere between December and February.
8. The Atlantic Ocean lies in the E̲astern part of the United States.
9. A good collection of young adult literature can be found at B̲aldwin p̲ublic library.
10. Black beans and spices are often found in S̲outhwestern cooking.

Try It

Scan a local newspaper looking for organizations and departments of government that use capital letters. Write down all that you find.

Answers will vary.

79

The titles of books, poems, songs, movies, plays, newspapers, and magazines are **proper nouns** and are capitalized. Most titles are also underlined in text. Song titles and essays, however, are in quotes.
book: *The Cat in the Hat*   song: *Atomic Dog*   magazine: *Time*

Titles associated with names are also capitalized.
Mayor Franklin   *Senator* Santos   *Professor* Johnson

Do not capitalize these titles if they are not directly used with the name.
The *mayor* of our town is *Mayor Franklin*.

Geographic names, such as the names of countries, states, cities, counties, bodies of water, public areas, roads and highways, and buildings are capitalized.
Columbia, Hawaii, Athens, Chesapeake Bay, Sierra Nevada Range, Rocky Mountain National Park, Paint Creek Trail, Globe Theatre

If the geographic name is not a specific name, do not capitalize it.
I'm going to *the lake* for the weekend.

Complete It

Complete the following sentences by circling the best answer in parentheses.

1. My favorite song is ("Vertigo") "vertigo") by U2.
2. The (President (president) of the organization is visiting on Tuesday.
3. At 2:00 pm, (Governor) governor) Spencer is making a speech.
4. Valerie and Gerald watched the sunset from the (Eiffel Tower) eiffel tower).
5. Are you going to the (Mountains (mountains) or the beach for vacation?
6. One of my favorite books is (The Elephant Hospital) the elephant hospital).
7. Lynda walks in a park along the (Scioto River) scioto river).
8. The (Martin Luther King, Jr. Highway) Martin Luther King, Jr. highway) is located in Washington, D.C.
9. My cousin was born in (Birmingham) birmingham), England.
10. The tiny (Village, (village) sits next to a canal.

80

Answer Key

Find It

Answer the following questions. If you need help, use an encyclopedia or other resource. Be sure to capitalize the answers when necessary.

1. Who is the principal of your school? _____
2. What city, state, and country do you live in? _____
3. Where were you born? _____
4. Who is the governor of your state? _____
5. What is your favorite book? _____
6. What is your favorit~~e~~   *Answers will vary.*
7. What is your favorit~~e~~
8. What states border the state in which you live? _____
9. What is the closest national park to where you live? _____
10. What is the name of your local newspaper? _____
11. What magazine do you like to read the most? _____
12. What is the name of one of your state s senators? _____

Try It

Use the information gathered above to write a brief biography about yourself. As in your previous answers, remember to capitalize titles and geographic names when necessary. You can also include other information about yourself in addition to the facts above.

Answers will vary.

81

The first word of every **sentence** is capitalized.
     The wind blew strongly through the trees.

The first word in **direct quotations** is also capitalized.
     My father said, *Finish* your homework and then we ll go for a ride.
     I m almost finished now, I happily answered.

Indirect quotations are not capitalized.
     My father said he had been working on his car for weeks.

If a continuous sentence in a direct quotation is split and the second half is not a new sentence, do not capitalize it. If a new sentence begins after the split, then capitalize it as you would with any sentence.
     Keep your hands and arms inside the car, said the attendant, *and* stay seated.
     Roller coasters are my favorite rides, I said. *I* can ride them all day.

Complete It

Complete the following sentences by circling the best answer in parentheses.

1. (The) the) girls team beat the boys team by three seconds.
2. T.C. said, (Baseball) baseball) is my favorite sport.
3. (Put) put) your donated clothing in plastic bags, said the event organizer.
4. The technician said (The,(the) car would be ready in a few hours.
5. Don t rush through your homework, said the teacher, (And,(and) stay focused.
6. Be careful as you shovel the snow, mother said. (You,) you) can hurt your back.
7. (The,) the) airplane was going to be delayed.
8. Renee said, (Would,) would) you like a baseball hat when we go to the park?
9. (Our,) our) race will begin in 10 minutes, said the announcer.
10. The sales clerk said (She,(she) would hold the item for one day.
11. Lemon cream is my favorite pie, said Lisa, (But,(but) nothing beats brownies.
12. I can t wait until my birthday, said Jack. (My,) my) parents are giving me a party.

82

Proof It

Proofread the following dialogue correcting capitalization errors.

| ^ | — inserts correct words or punctuation |
| = | — capitalize letter |

     Hi, Dad, said Jack. w̲e learned about tsunamis today.

     w̲hat did you learn about tsunamis? Jack's dad asked.

     Jack answered, w̲ell, we learned that tsunamis can move up to 500 miles per hour. w̲e also learned about how they are formed.

     T̲he earth s crust is made up of interlocking plates, said Jack. t̲he plates are floating on a hot, flexible interior that drifts. The plates sometimes collide. In a subduction, an ocean plate slides under continental plates. Over the years, the plates lock, the seafloor compresses, and the coastline warps up. e̲ventually, the pressure pops and the seafloor lunges landward. The coast lunges seaward. t̲he plates push seawater all over, creating the tsunami. Geologists can study sedimentary layers near the seaside to tell when shifts have occurred in the past, maybe helping to understand when it might happen again.

Try It

Write a dialogue between you and a friend, teacher, or parent. Explain to the other person something you learned about in school. Remember the capitalization rules.

Answers will vary.

83

A **personal letter** has five parts: heading, salutation, body, closing, and signature.

The **heading** of a personal letter is the address of the person writing the letter and the date it is written. The name of the street, the city, the state, and the month are all capitalized.
     1245 Hollow Dr.
     Suncrest, AZ
     March 31, 2008

The **salutation** is the greeting and begins with the word *dear*. Both *dear* and the name of the person who is receiving the letter are capitalized. The salutation ends with a comma.
     Dear Stanley,

The **body** is the main part of the letter and contains sentences that are capitalized as normal.

The **closing** can be written in many ways; only the first word is capitalized.
     Your friend,   Sincerely,   All the best,

The **signature** is usually only your first name in a personal letter. It is also always capitalized.
     Milton

Identify It

Identify the parts of the personal letter by writing the names on the lines provided. Then, circle the capital letters.

                                                  7511 Hibernia Rd.
          __heading__   Seattle, WA 40000
                                                  February 31, 2008

Dear Uncle Josh, ___salutation___

     How are you? My ski trip has been great. I even learned how to snowboard. I think I ll be really sore tomorrow. All of the fundraising was worth it. Thanks for helping us out. I m glad our class got to take this trip. I hope I ll get to come back someday. ___body___

                              Thank you, ___closing___
                              Mike ___signature___

84

Spectrum Language Arts
Grade 6

Page 85

A **business letter** has six parts: heading, inside address, salutation, body, closing and signature.

The **heading** of a business letter is the address of the person writing the letter and the date it is written. The name of the street, the city, the state, and the month are all capitalized.

4003 Fourteenth St.
Amlin, NH 20000
September 6, 2008

The **inside address** includes the name and complete address of the person to whom the letter is going.

Mark Dillon, Director
S.A.S Productions
100 Otterbein Ave.
Rochester, NY 20000

The **salutation** is the greeting and begins with the word *dear*. Both *dear* and the name of the person who is receiving the letter are capitalized. The salutation ends with a colon.

Dear Director:

The **body** is the main part of the letter and contains sentences that are capitalized as normal.

The **closing** can be written many ways. Only the first word is capitalized.

Yours truly,   Sincerely,   Very truly,

The **signature** is your full name and is capitalized.

Leigh D. McGregor

Try It

Write the heading, inside address, salutation, closing, and signature of a business letter. Make up the names and other information, but be sure you capitalize correctly.

heading: _____   inside address: _____

Answers will vary. Make sure capitalization is correct.

salutation: _____

signature: _____

85

Page 86

Review: Capitalization: Proper Nouns: Days of the Week; Months of the Year; Historical Events; Names of Languages and Nationalities; Team Names; Organizations; Departments of Government; Sections of the Country; Sentences; Direct Quotations

Putting It Together

Complete the following sentences by circling the best answer in parentheses.

1. Riley, called Gillian, (Let s, **Let s**) use carrots and raisins on our snowman.
2. Our teacher said the test will be on (**Wednesday,** wednesday).
3. (**Winters,** winters) in the north are cold and blustery.
4. The summer solstice occurs in the month of (**June,** june).
5. Drive (North, **north**) on Route 3 and then you ll be close to the community center.
6. The hostess said, (**Your,** your) table will be ready in 10 minutes.
7. The U.S. (**Constitution,** constitution) was drawn in Philadelphia in 1787.
8. The (**Peace Corp,** peace corp) is a federal agency that reports to Congress and the Executive Branch.
9. (**My,** my) shift starts at 3:00, so let s study when I m finished. said Celia.
10. The high school offers (**Italian,** italian) as one of its languages.
11. The (**Aveda Corporation,** aveda corporation) is located in Minnesota.
12. North America is located in the (Northern, **northern**) hemisphere.
13. In the fairy tale, the princess said (She, **she**) was waiting for her prince.
14. The (**Danish,** danish) pastry is baked fresh every day.
15. My favorite baseball team is the (**San Francisco Giants,** San Francisco giants).
16. The pep rally will be held in the gym on (**Friday,** friday) afternoon.
17. The (**Sierra Club,** sierra club) is an environmental organization for people of all ages.
18. Doug said, (**My,** my) Aunt Clara makes the best blueberry muffins.
19. Samuel <u>Adams and Paul</u> Revere were two of the colonists who initiated the events of the (**Boston Tea Party,** Boston tea party).
20. The winter solstice occurs in the month of (**December,** december).
21. The bus driver said (Traffic, **traffic**) was causing delays.
22. Surfing is popular on the (**North,** north) Coast of Oahu.

86

Page 87

Review: Capitalization: Personal Letters, Business Letters

Putting It Together

Proofread the following business letter. Make all necessary capitalization corrections.

= — capitalize letter

105 front street
Norfolk, VA 20000
april 17, 2008

Mr. Henry Munson, director
Student Volunteer Programs
242 W. 29th street
New York, NY 30000

dear Mr. Munson:

My name is John Burg and I am a seventh-grader at Houghton junior high school in Norfolk, Virginia. I would like to apply for a position with the Student Volunteer Save the Turtle Program.

I am on the basketball and track teams. I also write for our school paper. I am also a junior member of our local chapter of the sierra club. I have researched the Save the Turtle Program and would be honored to be a member of the upcoming team.

Included with this letter are my application and a list of references. I look forward to having a phone interview with you to further discuss your programs. thank you for your time.

sincerely,

John Burg

John Burg

87

Page 88

Sometimes, imperative sentences call for a **period**, as when the sentence is not urgent.

Pay the toll at the booth.

Periods are used in dialogue. The period goes inside the quotation mark.

Jean said, Give Mimi a drink of water.

If the quote comes at the beginning of the sentence, use a comma at the end of the direct quotation and before the quotation mark. Place a period at the end of the sentence.

If it gets cold, put on your jacket, said Robyn.

Use a period after each part of an abbreviation. Use a period after each letter of an initial.

M.A. (Master of Arts)   Samuel L. Jackson

Complete It

Complete the following sentences by adding periods where necessary.

1. Check out at the far counter
   Check out at the far counter.
2. Janet said, Let s take a long walk
   Janet said, Let s take a long walk.
3. Hiking is my favorite hobby, said Charlie
   Hiking is my favorite hobby, said Charlie.
4. Kathryn received her MA from the University of Arizona.
   Kathryn received her M.A. from the University of Arizona.
5. My favorite actress is Vivica A Fox.
   My favorite actress is Vivica A. Fox.
6. Jump over the puddle, so you will stay dry, yelled Eddie
   Jump over the puddle, so you will stay dry, yelled Eddie.
7. Reach a little farther, and you will have touched the top
   Reach a little farther, and you will have touched the top.
8. JRR Tolkein is my favorite author.
   J.R.R. Tolkein is my favorite author.

88

Answer Key

Page 89

Proof It
Proofread the following recipe. Add periods after imperative sentences and in abbreviations where they are necessary.

⊙ — inserts period

Homemade Hummus

4 cups cooked & drained garbanzo beans

1 cup tahini

1 cup fresh lemon juice

6 tbs.(tablespoons) olive oil

⅔ cup minced garlic

1 tsp.(teaspoon) salt

1 tsp.(teaspoon) black pepper

Place all ingredients in a large mixing bowl.Mash ingredients with a fork and then blend well.Store hummus covered in the refrigerator.Remove hummus from refrigerator when ready to serve.Sprinkle hummus with paprika Serve hummus at room temperature.

Recipe serves 12-15.

Try It
Write your favorite recipe. Don t forget the periods after abbreviations.

_____

_____

_____

_____
    Answers will vary.
_____

_____

_____

89

Page 90

Periods are used in more than just sentences and words. When used with numbers, periods are called **decimal points**.

Decimals are fractions with denominators of 10, 100, 1,000, etc. shown by decimal points before the numerators.
$$0.5 = \frac{5}{10} \qquad 0.25 = \frac{25}{100} \qquad 0.725 = \frac{725}{1000}$$

Decimal points are used in money with dollars and cents.
    $1.50   0.25 cents

Identify It
Write **D** on the line following each sentence that uses a decimal point in a decimal.
Write an **M** on the line following each sentence that uses a decimal point with money.
Write an **A** on the line following each sentence that uses periods with abbreviations.
Write an **I** on the line following each sentence that uses periods with initials.

1. The equivalent of 0.8 is $\frac{8}{10}$. __D__

2. The package cost $2.50 to mail. __M__

3. Rashad went to school for his B.S. degree. __A__

4. T.S. Eliot is a famous poet. __I__

5. The babysitter made $10.00 an hour. __M__

6. G. B. Shaw, an Irish playwright, was awarded the Nobel Prize in Literature in 1925. __I__

7. The equivalent of 0.78 is $\frac{78}{100}$. __D__

8. Mapleleaf Blvd. will be under construction for two weeks. __A__

9. The prize for first place is a $20.00 gift certificate. __M__

10. John F. Kennedy was the 35th President of the United States. __I__

11. Use 1 oz. of water. __A__

12. The equivalent of 0.123 is $\frac{123}{1000}$. __D__

90

Page 91

Solve It
Express the following fractions as decimals.

1. $\frac{3}{10}$ = _0.3_

2. $\frac{4}{10}$ = _0.4_

3. $\frac{9}{100}$ = _0.09_

4. $\frac{8}{10}$ = _0.8_

5. $\frac{6}{10}$ = _0.6_

Try It
Write a sentence for each answer above. The first one has been done for you.

1. _Camden ate 0.3 of the pizza already!_

2. _____

3. _____
    Answers will vary.
4. _____

5. _____

91

Page 92

Question marks are used in sentences that ask questions, called interrogative sentences.
    How was your trip?

When used in quotations, questions marks can be placed either inside or outside of the end quotation mark depending on the meaning of the sentence.

When the question mark is punctuating the quotation itself, it is placed inside the quote.
    The coach asked, How many push-ups can you do?

When the question mark is punctuating the entire sentence, it is placed outside the quote.
    Did the coach say, Try to do twice as many as you did last week ?

A question mark is not used in sentences with indirect quotations.
    Suhad asked the librarian for help finding the book.

Match It
Draw a line to match the sentences in Column A with their descriptions in Column B.

Column A	Column B
1. Bill asked the guide how long the museum would be open.	interrogative sentence
2. Could you tell that funny joke again?	question mark punctuating quotation
3. Sylvia s mother asked, What time is your track meet on Saturday?	question mark punctuating entire sentence
4. Did the weather reporter say, Expect six inches of snow tonight ?	indirect quotation
5. Where did you park the car?	interrogative sentence
6. Did you say, Read page four ?	question mark punctuating quotation
7. Sam asked for a quarter to make a wish in the well.	question mark punctuating entire sentence
8. The teacher asked, What is the square root of 64?	indirect quotation

92

Answer Key

Proof It
Proofread the following dialogue correcting the misplaced and misused question marks.

> ∨ — inserts quotations
> ↶ —moves letters, words, punctuation, text from one location to another

Dr. Edwards, asked Eric, what should I study in school if I want to be a vet?

Dr. Edwards answered, Eric, anyone who wants to be a vet should study math and science. Veterinarians have to go to medical school, just like people doctors. They have to know how much and which medicines to prescribe. Dr. Edwards continued, You must also be good at social skills.

I like working with people. Is that important? asked Eric.

Oh, yes, exclaimed Dr. Edwards. Doctors have to listen to their patients. In this case, the patients guardians have to speak for them. I listen very carefully to help with my diagnosis. Sometimes, vets have to discuss serious matters with the guardians.

Eric asked the doctor what was the most important quality for a vet to possess.

Veterinarians must love animals, answered Dr. Edwards. We care for them and their guardians in the very best way we can. Do you still want to be a vet, Eric?

Absolutely! answered Eric.

Try It
Write three sentences using question marks: one interrogative sentence, one sentence where the question mark punctuates the quotation, and one sentence where the question mark punctuates the entire sentence.

_____

Answers will vary.

93

Exclamation points are used at the end of sentences that express surprise and strong emotion, called exclamatory sentences.
> We have to read all three chapters for homework!

Interjections sometimes require exclamation points.
> Ah ha! I ve come up with the answer!

If you use an exclamation point, make sure the sentence expresses surprise, urgency, or strong emotion. Don t overuse exclamation points.

Complete It
Complete the following sentences by circling the best end punctuation in parentheses.

1. Can bees talk (.**?**)
2. Scientists have discovered that bees do communicate with each other (.**!**)
3. How do they talk (**?**!)
4. Bees don t talk with their voices (.**!**)
5. Bees talk through dance (?**!**)
6. What do bees talk about (.**?**)
7. Bees talk about gathering food (**.**!)
8. One dance move tells where the food is located (**.**?)
9. Another dance move tells how far the food is away (**.**!)
10. Are there more dance moves (**?**!)
11. Yes, another move tells about how much food is in a particular location (**.**?)
12. Do dancing bees have a special name (**?**!)
13. The bees who communicate about the food are called scout bees (**.**!)
14. Scout bees dance for forager bees (**.**?)
15. Forager bees interpret the dance and go out to get the food (**.**?)
16. How do the forager bees understand what the moves mean (**?**!)
17. How fast the scouts dance tells how far the food is away (**.**?)
18. The angle the scouts dance tells where the food is and the number of times the scouts dance tells how much food there is (**.**?)
19. What an amazing story (?**!**)
20. Bees are amazing creatures (.**!**)

Answers may vary.

94

Solve It
Choose a word from the box to complete the following sentences so they express strong emotion or surprise. Not all words will be used.

brave	fast	loud	show	tall
cautious	freezing	low	short	tied
close	high	luke warm	soft	warm
far	hot	mild	spicy	won

1. Don t touch the stove, it is ____hot____!
2. Look how ____fast____ that racecar driver took the curve!
3. Please turn down that ____loud____ music!
4. The trapeze performer is so ____high____ from the ground!
5. This tour through the caves is scary; the walls are too ____close____!
6. It s cold outside and the water is ____freezing____!
7. The astronauts on this mission are so ____brave____!
8. Be careful when you take a bite, the dip is very ____spicy____!
9. Yea! Our team ____won____ the championship!
10. The sequoia tree is so ____tall____!

Try It
Write a paragraph describing an exciting sporting event in which you participated or watched. Use exclamation points where appropriate.

_____

Answers will vary.

95

Commas have a variety of uses, such as in a series, in direct address, and with multiple adjectives.

Series commas are used when there is at least three items listed in a sentence in a row. The items can be words or phrases. Commas are used to separate them.
> My favorite foods are *pizza, pasta salad, and vegetable burritos.*
> To make a pizza you have to *roll the crust, spread the sauce, and add the toppings.*

Commas are used to separate the name of a person spoken to from the rest of the sentence. This is called a **direct address**.
> *Ken,* please answer the door.   Your delivery has arrived, *Adam.*

When more than one adjective is used to describe a noun, they are separated by commas.
> It was a *warm, breezy* day.

Make sure the adjectives equally modify the noun, and that one item is not actually an adverb modifying the adjective. There is no comma in the following sentence because *hilariously* is an adverb modifying *funny,* not *book.*
> Calvin read a *hilariously funny* book.

Identify It
Write an **S** for series, a **DA** for direct address, or an **MA** for multiple adjectives.

1. __S__ Before you leave for school, eat your breakfast, put your homework in your backpack, and brush your teeth.
2. __MA__ I had a sweet, juicy apple for lunch.
3. __DA__ Finish your homework before playing video games, Craig.
4. __MA__ Shawn had a long, hard homework assignment.
5. __DA__ Chloe, your song in the concert was beautiful.
6. __S__ Don t forget your maps, food, and water for your hiking trip.
7. __DA__ Trevor, wash your hands before dinner.
8. __S__ I grabbed a book, paper, and a pencil from my desk when packing for our trip.
9. __MA__ It was a cold, blustery day.

96

Answer Key

Proof It
Rewrite the following dialogue, adding commas where they are needed.

↑ — inserts a comma

Reese ↑ guess what I m doing this weekend, said Dani.

Are you going to play basketball at the school ↑ clean your room at home ↑ or finish your science report? answered Reese.

None of the above, Reese ↑ Dani said grinning. I m going to the best ↑ brightest show on the planet. My grandparents are taking me to see Cirque du Soleil.

Reese replied, Isn t that the circus with only human performers?

Yep, that s the one, answered Dani. The brave ↑ talented acrobats do all kinds of maneuvers high in the air on ropes. They dance ↑ swing and fly through the air.

I think I even heard that they do some acts underwater! said Reese.

They also have hysterically funny clowns, added Dani. I ve heard that sometimes they even spray water on the audience!

I ve got a nice ↑ big surprise for you ↑ Reese, beamed Dani. My grandparents got tickets for you ↑ your brother and your sister.

I hope we re sitting in the front row, shouted Reese, even if we do get wet!

Try It
Write six sentences of our own. Write two sentences with series, two with direct addresses, and two with multiple adjectives.

1. _____
2. _____
3. _____
4. ____ Answers will vary. ____
5. _____
6. _____

97

Simple sentences may become more interesting when they are combined into compound or complex sentences. Sometimes, this means using **commas**.

Use a comma to combine two independent clauses with a coordinate conjunction. The student must read three chapters, *and* answer the questions at the end of each chapter.

When combining an independent clause to a dependent clause (a complex sentence) use a comma. The clauses are connected with a comma and subordinate conjunction.
Although the skies were sunny now, clouds were rolling in.

Commas are used when setting off dialogue from the rest of the sentence.
The salesperson said, *Our gym has classes in aerobics, kickboxing, and cycling.*

Match It
Draw an arrow to connect the sentences in Column A with the types of sentences in Column B.

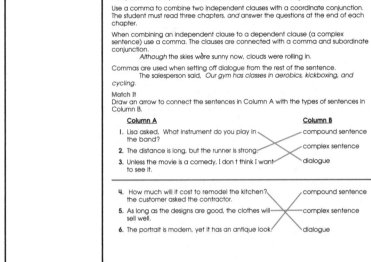

Column A	Column B
1. Lisa asked, What instrument do you play in the band?	compound sentence
2. The distance is long, but the runner is strong.	complex sentence
3. Unless the movie is a comedy, I don t think I want to see it.	dialogue

4. How much will it cost to remodel the kitchen? the customer asked the contractor.	compound sentence
5. As long as the designs are good, the clothes will sell well.	complex sentence
6. The portrait is modern, yet it has an antique look.	dialogue

98

Proof It
Proofread the following biography. Add or delete commas as necessary.

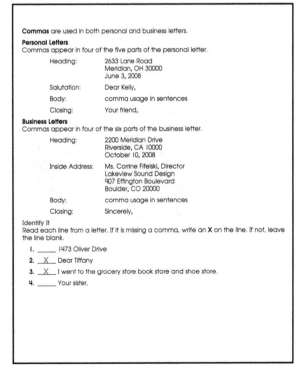

| ℓ — deletes incorrect letters, words, punctuation |
| ↑ — inserts a comma |

Arthur Ashe

Arthur Ashe was born in Richmond, Virginia in 1943. He started playing tennis when he was seven years old. Although the field was dominated by white athletes ↑ Ashe won many amateur titles in his teenage years. He won a scholarship to UCLA and during college competed in Wimbledon for the first time.

Ashe continued to win many major titles. In 1968 ↑ he won the U.S. Open ↑ becoming the top male ranked player in the United States Lawn Tennis Association. Until 1973 ↑ no African American had been permitted to compete in the South African tournament ↑ Ashe became the first. He went on to win Wimbledon and the World Championship of Tennis. He was the top ranked tennis player in the world in 1975.

A heart attack in 1979 forced him to retire in 1980. In 1988, Ashe suffered a devastating blow when he discovered he had contracted AIDS from a previous heart operation. Ashe was terminally ill, but he remained an active spokesperson for race relations and AIDS. Arthur Ashe died in February 1993.

Try It
Write three sentences with commas of your own: one in a compound sentence, one in a complex sentence, and one with a quotation.

_____
_____
____ Answers will vary. ____
_____

99

Commas are used in both personal and business letters.

Personal Letters
Commas appear in four of the five parts of the personal letter.

Heading:	2633 Lane Road Meridian, OH 30000 June 3, 2008
Salutation:	Dear Kelly,
Body:	comma usage in sentences
Closing:	Your friend,

Business Letters
Commas appear in four of the six parts of the business letter.

Heading:	2200 Meridian Drive Riverside, CA 10000 October 10, 2008
Inside Address:	Ms. Corrine Fifelski, Director Lakeview Sound Design 907 Effington Boulevard Boulder, CO 20000
Body:	comma usage in sentences
Closing:	Sincerely,

Identify It
Read each line from a letter. If it is missing a comma, write an **X** on the line. If not, leave the line blank.

1. _____ 1473 Oliver Drive
2. __X__ Dear Tiffany
3. __X__ I went to the grocery store book store and shoe store.
4. _____ Your sister,

100

Answer Key

---

927 Cobblestone Road
Buffalo NY 50000
September 3 2008

Dear Mimi

How are you? I hope you had a great summer vacation. I saw something fantastic on my trip to visit my grandparents in Japan. Do you remember studying about World War II in history class? Well I got to see an actual living relic from World War II. In the middle of Tokyo there is a tree that was hit with a bomb. Remarkably, the tree survived! We saw lots of fascinating things on our trip through Japan, but the tree was my favorite. I can t wait to see you on your next trip to Buffalo and show you the pictures. I even brought you back a special souvenir, a *maneki neko* cat. This means *beckoning cat,* and it's a lucky charm in Japan.

Your friend

Akira

---

927 Cobblestone Road

Buffalo, NY 50000

September 3, 2006

Dear Mimi,

How are you? I hope you had a great summer vacation. I saw something

fantastic on my trip to visit my grandparents in Japan. Do you remember studying

about World War II in history class? Well, I got to see an actual, living relic from

World War II. In the middle of Tokyo there is a tree that was hit with a bomb.

Remarkably, the tree survived! We saw lots of fascinating things on our trip through

Japan, but the tree was my favorite. I can t wait to see you on your next trip to

Buffalo and show you the pictures. I even brought you back a special souvenir, a

maneki neko cat. This means beckoning cat, and it's a lucky charm in Japan.

Your friend,

Akira

101

Quotation marks are used to show the exact words of a speaker. The quotation marks are placed before and after the exact words.
> Let s go to the movies tonight, said Janice. *The new action adventure was released.*

Quotation marks are also used when a direct quotation is made within a direct quotation. In this case, single quotation marks are used to set off the inside quotation.
> John said, Miss Robinson clearly said, *The project is due tomorrow.*

Single quotes express what Miss Robinson said. Double quotes express what John said.

Quotation marks are used with some titles. Quotation marks are used with the titles of short stories, poems, songs, and articles in magazines and newspapers.
> *North Carolina Takes the Championship* — newspaper article

If a title is quoted within a direct quotation, then single quotation marks are used.
> Melissa said, Did you read the article *Saving Our Oceans* in the magazine?

Identify It
On the lines, write a **DQ** for direct quote, a **QQ** for quote within quote, a **T** for title, and a **TQ** for title in quote.

1. _DQ_ Sandra shouted, Our team won the game!
2. _QQ_ Suzie responded, I heard the coach say, This was my best team ever!
3. _T_ The magazine <u>Sports Today</u> had an article called "A Winning Season."
4. _TQ_ What did the article A Winning Season say about our team? Sandra asked.
5. _DQ_ The writer of the article thinks we could win the championship, Suzie said.
6. _QQ_ He said, The team is strong offensively and defensively and could go all the way, continued Suzie.
7. _DQ_ This is so exciting, yelled Sandra.
8. _TQ_ Suzie said, Let s go check out our newspaper Community Times and see what they had to say!

102

Rewrite It
Rewrite the following list of famous quotations, adding quotation marks where they are needed.

1. Arthur Ashe said, From what we get, we can make a living; what we give, however, makes a life.

   Arthur Ashe said, "From what we get, we
   can make a living; what we give, however,
   makes a life.

2. The most important thing is not to stop questioning, said Albert Einstein.

   The most important thing is not to stop questioning, said Albert Einstein.

3. Mahatma Ghandi said, The weak can never forgive. Forgiveness is the attribute of the strong.

   Mahatma Ghandi said, The weak can never forgive. Forgiveness is the attribute of the strong.

4. Although the world is full of suffering, it is full also of the overcoming of it, said Helen Keller.

   Although the world is full of suffering, it is full also of the overcoming of it, said Helen Keller.

Try It
Write two sentences of dialogue that include direct quotations by characters. Write two sentences that include a title. Write two direct quotations of your own.

Answers will vary.
Make sure quotations are appropriately placed.

103

Apostrophes are used in contractions, to form possessives, and to form plurals.

Contractions are shortened forms of words. The words are shorted by leaving out letters. Apostrophes take the place of the omitted letters.
> he is = he s   can not = can t

Possessives show possession, or ownership. To form the possessive of a singular noun, add an apostrophe and an **s**.
> I ll carry *Harry s* notebook.

To form the possessive of plural nouns ending in **s**, simply add the apostrophe. If the plural noun does not end in an **s**, add both the apostrophe and an **s**.
> The *puppies* guardians are very happy.
> The *women s* team has won every game.

Match It
The sentences in Column A contain words with apostrophes. Match these sentences to the types of apostrophes used in Column B. Draw an arrow to make your match.

Column A	Column B
1. Felicia s jacket is in my car.	contraction
2. She s my best friend.	singular possessive
3. The men s shirts are on the second floor.	plural possessive ending in **s**
4. The girls tickets are at the box office.	plural possessive not ending in **s**

Column A	Column B
5. The parents cars lined the street.	contraction
6. Patty s blanket is nearly done.	singular possessive
7. The children s toys are in the toy box.	plural possessive ending in **s**
8. Teddy s got the presentation.	plural possessive not ending in **s**

104

Answer Key

Complete It
Complete the following sentences by circling the best answer in parentheses.

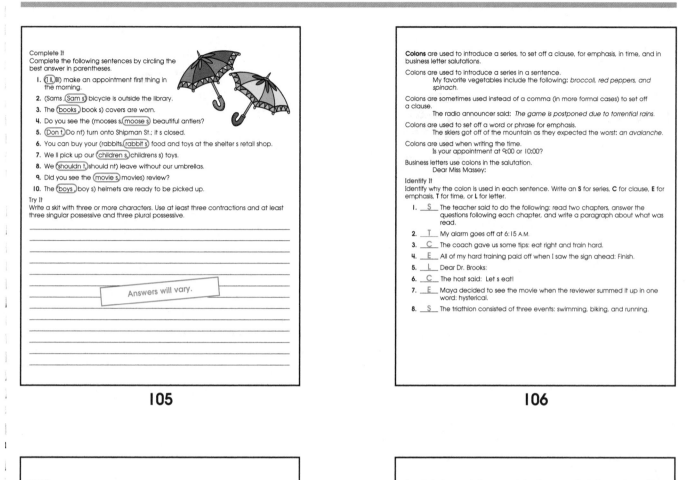

1. (I'll, Il, Ill) make an appointment first thing in the morning.
2. (Sams, Sam's) bicycle is outside the library.
3. The (books, book s) covers are worn.
4. Do you see the (mooses s, moose's) beautiful antlers?
5. (Don't, Do nt) turn onto Shipman St.; it's closed.
6. You can buy your (rabbits, rabbit's) food and toys at the shelter s retail shop.
7. We'll pick up our (children's, childrens s) toys.
8. We (shouldn't, should nt) leave without our umbrellas.
9. Did you see the (movie's, movies) review?
10. The (boys', boy s) helmets are ready to be picked up.

Try It
Write a skit with three or more characters. Use at least three contractions and at least three singular possessive and three plural possessive.

Answers will vary.

105

Colons are used to introduce a series, to set off a clause, for emphasis, in time, and in business letter salutations.

Colons are used to introduce a series in a sentence.
    My favorite vegetables include the following: *broccoli, red peppers, and spinach.*

Colons are sometimes used instead of a comma (in more formal cases) to set off a clause.
    The radio announcer said: *The game is postponed due to torrential rains.*

Colons are used to set off a word or phrase for emphasis.
    The skiers got off of the mountain as they expected the worst: *an avalanche.*

Colons are used when writing the time.
    Is your appointment at 9:00 or 10:00?

Business letters use colons in the salutation.
    Dear Miss Massey:

Identify It
Identify why the colon is used in each sentence. Write an **S** for series, **C** for clause, **E** for emphasis, **T** for time, or **L** for letter.

1. __S__ The teacher said to do the following: read two chapters, answer the questions following each chapter, and write a paragraph about what was read.
2. __T__ My alarm goes off at 6:15 A.M.
3. __C__ The coach gave us some tips: eat right and train hard.
4. __E__ All of my hard training paid off when I saw the sign ahead: Finish.
5. __L__ Dear Dr. Brooks:
6. __C__ The host said: Let s eat!
7. __E__ Maya decided to see the movie when the reviewer summed it up in one word: hysterical.
8. __S__ The triathlon consisted of three events: swimming, biking, and running.

106

Proof It
Proofread the following dialogue. Add colons where needed.

    ⁝ — inserts colon

Hurry up, Henry, it s almost 1:00. We want to get to the animal shelter soon, shouted Mrs. Knapp.

I'm glad we re adopting from a shelter, Mom. There are so many dogs, cats, and other animals who don t have homes, Henry said.

You re right, Henry, said Mrs. Knapp. There are many reasons to adopt from a shelter: it saves animals' lives, the animals have all been seen by a vet, and the animals are spayed and neutered.

"I can't wait to see Ginger, said Henry, and tell her she is coming home with us! The shelter director told me: I'm so glad you are adopting an older dog. Older pets need homes just like the little ones.

"Well, we better get going, Henry, said Mrs. Knapp. It's almost 1:15, and we need to pick up some dog toys on the way there!"

Try It
Write four sentences with colons: one that introduces a series, one used with a clause, one that expresses emphasis, and one used with time.

Answers will vary.

107

A **semicolon** is a cross between a period and a comma. Semicolons can be used to join two independent clauses, to separate clauses containing commas, and to separate groups which contain commas.

Semicolons join two independent clauses when a coordinate conjunction is not used.
    The city s sounds are loud; I love the excitement.

Semicolons are used to separate clauses when they already contain commas.
    After the sun sets, the lights come on; the city is beautiful at night.

Semicolons are also used to separate words or phrases that already contain commas.
    Billi s new apartment has a bedroom for her, her sister, and her brother; a laundry room; an exercise room; and a game room.

Rewrite It
Rewrite the following sentences adding semicolons where needed.

1. The insulation in the room wasn t very effective it was freezing.
   <u>The insulation in the room wasn t very affective; it was freezing.</u>

2. Although we were relieved it didn t rain, we needed it a drought was upon us.
   <u>Although we were relieved it didn t rain, we needed it; a drought was upon us.</u>

3. They needed equipment to start a business computer monitor printer and furniture, such as desks, chairs, and lamps.
   <u>The needed equipment to start a business; computer; monitor; printer; and furniture, such as desks, chairs, and lamps.</u>

4. Riana has the aptitude for science it is her favorite subject.
   <u>Riana has the aptitude for science; it is her favorite subject.</u>

5. Since the opening is delayed, we ll shop on Tuesday I m looking forward to it.
   <u>Since the opening is delayed, we ll shop on Tuesday; I m looking forward to it.</u>

108

Answer Key

Page 109

Solve It
Look at the following pictures. The scenes depicted complete the sentences below. Write the conclusion to each sentence by interpreting and matching them to a picture. Remember to add semicolons where they are needed in your completed sentences. Rewrite the entire sentence.

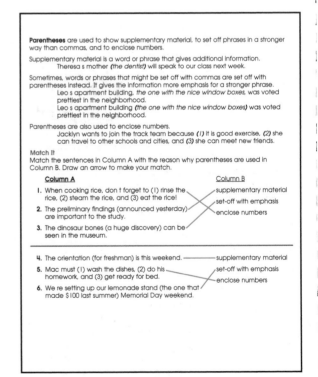

Answers will vary, possible responses given. Accept all reasonable answers.

Sentences

1. _____The building was so tall_____ it soared beyond the clouds.
   The building was so tall; it soared beyond the clouds.

2. Although the score was tied, our team looked strong_ the crowd cheered us on,_.
   Although the score was tied, our team looked strong; the crowd cheered us on.

3. The movie had all of the right parts: actors who were young, rich, and good looking; action that was fast, furious, and suspenseful; and music that was loud and motivating.
   The movie had all the right parts: actors who were young, rich, and good looking; action that was fast, furious, and suspenseful; and music that was loud and motivating.

Try It
Write a review of a movie you have seen or a book you have read. Include at least two of the following uses of semicolons: between independent clauses, to separate clauses that contain clauses, and to separate words that contain commas.

Answers will vary.

109

Page 110

Hyphens are used to divide words, to create new words, and are used between numbers.

Use a hyphen to divide the word between syllables.
beau-ti-ful   per-form

Do not divide one-syllable words with fewer than six letters.
through   piece

Do not divide one letter from the rest of the word.
event-ful   not: e-ventful

Divide syllables after the vowel if the vowel is a syllable by itself.
come-dy   not: com-edy

Divide words with double consonants between the consonants.
swim-ming   mir-ror

Hyphens can be used to create new words when combined with *self*, *ex*, and *great*. The pianist was self-taught.

Hyphens are used between numbers.
twenty-one

Complete It
Choose the best word in parentheses to complete each sentence.

1. Next year I ll pick an (instru-ment, instr-ument) to play in the band.
2. Julia burned her (ton-gue, tongue) on the hot chocolate.
3. An (o-ceanographer, ocean-ographer) studies the oceans and the plants and animals that live in them.
4. My (ex-coach, excoach) won teacher of the year.
5. The glass holds (thirty two, thirty-two) ounces.
6. The students are raising money for their chosen (char-ity, chari-ty).
7. Armonite would like a (ch-air, chair) for her bedroom.
8. The clock seems to be (run-ning, runn-ing) fast.
9. Richard s (great aunt, great-aunt) bakes the best blackberry pie.
10. Her jersey number is (sixty-four, sixty four).

110

Page 111

Hyphenate It
One word in each sentence... complete the word using a hyphen...

Some answers may be divided in more than one way. Accept all correct answers.

1. The longest one syllable word in the English language is screeched.
   long-est
2. Dreamt is the only English word that ends in the letters mt. ___let-ters
3. In the 18th and 19th centuries, doctors used leaches to treat headaches. ___leach-es
4. No two lions have the same pattern of whiskers in their muzzles.
   whis-kers
5. Bats are the only mammals that can fly. ___mam-mals
6. Basketball star Shaquille O Neal wears size 22 shoes. ___basket-ball
7. Ann Meyers was the first female player to sign a contract with an NBA team.
   fe-male
8. The average lifespan of a major league baseball is seven pitches. ___league

Try It
Use a dictionary to look up two words with the prefix **ex-**, two words with the prefix **great-**, and two words with the prefix **self-**. Write a sentence for each.

1. _____
2. _____
3. _____
   Answers will vary.
4. _____
5. _____
6. _____

111

Page 112

Parentheses are used to show supplementary material, to set off phrases in a stronger way than commas, and to enclose numbers.

Supplementary material is a word or phrase that gives additional information.
Theresa s mother *(the dentist)* will speak to our class next week.

Sometimes, words or phrases that might be set off with commas are set off with parentheses instead. It gives the information more emphasis for a stronger phrase.
Leo s apartment building, *the one with the nice window boxes*, was voted prettiest in the neighborhood.
Leo s apartment building *(the one with the nice window boxes)* was voted prettiest in the neighborhood.

Parentheses are also used to enclose numbers.
Jacklyn wants to join the track team because *(1)* it is good exercise, *(2)* she can travel to other schools and cities, and *(3)* she can meet new friends.

Match It
Match the sentences in Column A with the reason why parentheses are used in Column B. Draw an arrow to make your match.

Column A	Column B
1. When cooking rice, don t forget to (1) rinse the rice, (2) steam the rice, and (3) eat the rice!	supplementary material
2. The preliminary findings (announced yesterday) are important to the study.	set-off with emphasis
3. The dinosaur bones (a huge discovery) can be seen in the museum.	enclose numbers

4. The orientation (for freshman) is this weekend.	supplementary material
5. Mac must (1) wash the dishes, (2) do his homework, and (3) get ready for bed.	set-off with emphasis
6. We re setting up our lemonade stand (the one that made $100 last summer) Memorial Day weekend.	enclose numbers

112

Answer Key

Page 113

Rewrite It
Rewrite the following paragraph, adding parentheses where necessary.

Special Olympics

The Special Olympics were founded with the knowledge that people with intellectual disabilities can learn, participate, and enjoy sports. Eunice Kennedy Shriver started a day camp sports included for people with intellectual disabilities. Her sister was one of the first participants. She realized how important playing sports was to the people at her camps. In 1968, she organized the first ~~al Olympics~~ Games. One thousand ~~The placement of parentheses may vary in~~ ated. Today, both summer a ~~some instances, possible answers given.~~ from more than 150 count ~~Accept all reasonable answers.~~ coaching, volunteering, or ~~he games~~ continue to grow and attract athletes ~~for the world!~~

Special Olympics

The Special Olympics were founded with the knowledge that people with intellectual disabilities can (1) learn, (2) participate, and (3) enjoy sports. Eunice Kennedy Shriver started a day camp (sports included) for people with intellectual disabilities. Her sister was one of the first participants. She realized how important playing sports was to the people at her camps. In 1968, she organized the first International Special Olympics Games. One thousand athletes (from 26 U.S. states and Canada) participated. Today, both summer and winter World Games are held with over 1,800 athletes (from more than 150 countries) participating. Thousands support Special Olympics by (1) coaching, (2) volunteering, or (3) cheering on the committed athletes. The games continue to grow and attract athletes from all over the world!

Try It
Write three sentences about your favorite sporting event, either as a participant or a spectator. Use each of the three types of parentheses in your sentence.

1. _____
2. _____ Answers will vary.
3. _____

113

Page 114

Review: Periods: After Imperative Sentences, In Dialogue, In Abbreviations, In Initials, In Decimals, In Money; Question Marks, Exclamation Points

Putting It Together
Complete the following sentences by adding periods, question marks, and exclamation points where needed.

1. Marsha, called A.J., I heard you got your driver's license.
2. Washington DC is the capital of the United States.
3. The equivalent of ⅜ is ⅝.?
4. The customer asked, What comes on the garden salad?
5. Wow! That was the best movie I've ever seen!

Review: Commas: In a Series, Multiple Adjectives, Between Clauses, In Business Letters

Add commas in the appropriate places in the business letter.

1151 Davidson Street
Chicago, IL 40000
April 8, 2008

Mrs. Jane Merrinan, Director
City Community Center
1200 Adams Street
Chicago, IL 30000

Dear Mrs. Merrinan:

My name is A.J. Byington. I am interested in applying as a summer counselor at the Civic Community Center and as a part-time volunteer during the school year. I am a freshman at Northwest High School. My experience has included tutoring, coaching, and counseling students in elementary school. Your varied, well-rounded programs interest me. I have included my activities list and references. I look forward to talking with you in the near future. Thank you for your time.

Sincerely,

A.J. Byington
A.J. Byington

114

Page 115

Review: Commas: In Direct Address, Set-Off Dialogue; Quotation Marks; Apostrophes; Colons; Semicolons; Hyphens; Parentheses

Putting It Together
Proof the following para ~~Answers will vary.~~ marks, apostrophes, colons, semicolons, hyph ~~where needed.~~

"Sharon, are you going to the community center after school?" asked Susan.

"Yes, I'm going right after school to play some basketball; our team is going to the tournament. My greatgrandpa is going to cheer me on," answered Sharon.

"I'm so glad we have a center," said Sharon. "We learned in school about the very first community center. It was started by two very brave women, Jane Addams and Ellen Gates Starr."

Susan responded, "I don't think I've heard of them."

"They lived way back in the 1800s. Life in cities was not easy," Sharon continued. "Thousands of people worked in factories (even kids) and received little money in return. Jane and Ellen both wanted to help people. They moved into one of the worst parts of town. They found a big house on Halstead Street. They rented it and turned it into the first community center, Hall House. Hall House offered child care for working mothers (eventually leading to kindergarten classes). After awhile, many classes were offered to people of all ages: art, music, drama, cooking, science, math, and languages. The people of the city were finally brought together in a place where they could socialize, relax, and escape their working lives," responded Sharon. "Many of the people who came to Hall House went on to lead successful lives who helped other people."

"Well, Susan," said Sharon, "today's game will be played in honor of Jane Addams and Ellen Gates Starr!"

115

Page 116

The **present tense** of a verb tells that the action is taking place now or continuously.
   I *rise* at 6:00 every morning.
   Rona and Michael both *teach* third grade.
   Mimi and Chuck *write* well for kindergartners.

The **past tense** of a verb tells that the action took place in the past.
   I *rose* at 6:30 yesterday morning.
   A substitute *taught* our English class this morning.
   Robyn *wrote* her descriptive paragraph at the coffee shop.

The **past participle** of a verb tells that the action began in the past and was completed in the past. In order to form the past participle, the verb must be preceded by one of the following verbs: *was, were, has, had,* or *have.*
   Rachel *had risen* every day at the same time, until she got the flu.
   Mrs. Khory *has taught* our English class in the past.
   Jean *has written* her paper four times and is still not satisfied with it.

Match It
Draw a line to match the sentences in Column A with the words they are missing in Column B.

Column A

1. Greg and Lisa ____teach____ martial arts at the YMCA.
2. My grandmother had ____written____ her recipe down before I even asked her.
3. The sun has ____risen____ a little earlier every morning.
4. Mr. Lee had ____taught____ at the same school for 30 years before he retired.
5. I ____wrote____ a note for my mom and left it on the refrigerator.
6. The sun ____rose____ at 6:30 A.M. sharp.
7. Sasha ____taught____ us how to double jump rope during recess yesterday.
8. Ryan and Jaime ____write____ nice poetry.
9. Kurt and Perry ____rise____ at dawn.

Column B

rise
rose
risen
teach
taught
taught
write
wrote
written

116

Complete It
Circle the correct usage of the verbs *rise*, *teach*, and *write*.

Much has been (**written**, wrote) about our world s waterways. Novelists and poets (written, (**wrote**) about beautiful oceans, seas, and rivers. Some writers (risen, (**rise**) at dawn for the inspiration a sunrise can bring. But our waterways may not always be that inspiring, unless we step in and do something about it.

The famous explorer Jacque Cousteau and many other conservationists have ((**taught**, teach) us many lessons on ocean conservation. Our oceans and the marine life that inhabit them are at risk from many sources. Previous oil spills have (teach, (**taught**) us that we must take safer measures when transporting oil.

Conservationists are people who take action to help protect the things they love. They (risen, (**rise**) up and let their voices be heard. People who have ((**risen**, rose) in the past have noticed a change: a change for the better. New methods of oil transportation are being discussed, as well as oil clean-ups. Better ways to dispose of waste are being developed.

You can have your voice heard. You can (wrote, (**write**) letters to government officials asking for better laws to save our waterways. You can volunteer to help clean trash and litter from oceans and rivers. One of the most important things you can do is ((**teach**, taught) those around you about the importance of our oceans and marine life and how to keep them safe for everyone to enjoy for years and years to come.

Try It
Do you have a cause that is important to you? Write a letter to your local government official expressing your concerns. Include at least two of the verb forms from this lesson.

Answers will vary.

117

The irregular verbs *bring* and *take* are often confused with each other. When you *bring* something, it is coming in or toward you. When you *take* something, it is moving away.

The present tense of a verb tells that the action is taking place now or continuously.
The teacher asked her students to *bring* in newspapers.
The teacher asked her students to *take* books home.

The past tense of a verb tells that the action took place in the past.
Jessica *brought* her books home.
Jessica *took* magazines to her sick friend.

The past participle of a verb tells that the action began in the past and was completed in the past. In order to form the past participle, the verb must be preceded by one of the following verbs: *was, were, has, had* or *have.*
He *had brought* the tickets over just before we left.
He *had taken* the tickets to the game.

Complete It
Complete the following sentences by circling the best answers in parentheses.

1. Don t (bring, (**take**) the library books out of the building.
2. Vicki and Anna ((**bring**, brought) friends home every day after school.
3. Brian and Matt ((**take**, taken) extra water to the baseball games.
4. Last year Lilly (bring, (**brought**) cupcakes on her birthday.
5. Grover (brought, (**took**) six cookies out of the box.
6. Yesterday, we (take, (**took**) blankets and towels to the animal shelter.
7. The children were (bring, (**brought**) home when it started to thunder.
8. Marv was (took, (**taken**) to the hospital when he sprained his ankle.
9. Grandma said, Aubrey, ((**bring**, take) me a glass of water, please.
10. Charlie (brought, (**took**) seeds from his own garden to plant new flowers in the park.

118

Solve It
Choose the correct form of the verbs *bring* and *take* and complete the puzzle.

Across
2. Trisha had (**brought**, bring) everyone s favorite blueberry muffins to every meeting.
4. Adam and Mandy (**take**, bring) their puppy when they come for a visit.
5. Becky had (**taken**, take) flowers to the hospital every weekend for two years.

Down
1. Lisa and Dave (take, **bring**) meals to the elderly every evening.
2. Harold (brought, **bring**) his favorite book to read in the car.
3. Jake (bring, **took**) his cat to the vet for a check-up.

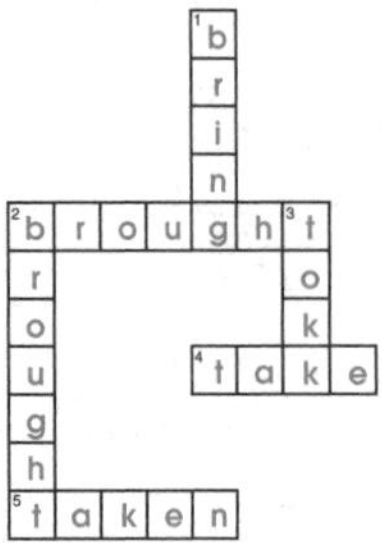

(crossword grid: 1 Down "bring"; 2 Across "brought"; 4 Across "take"; 5 Across "taken")

Try It
Write a letter to a friend or relative, using different forms of the verbs bring and take. Write about things that you either *bring* or *take* to or from school or home.

Answers will vary.

119

The irregular verbs *lay* and *lie* are easily confused.

The verb *lay* means *to place.*
The forms of the verb *lay* are *lay, laid,* and *laid.*

The verb *lie* means *to recline.*
The forms of the verb *lie* are *lie, lay,* and *lain.*

The present tense of a verb tells that the action is taking place now or continuously.
The teachers *lay* the papers on their desks.
The kittens *lie* by the window in the sun.

The past tense of a verb tells that the action took place in the past.
Bobby *laid* his homework on the kitchen table.
Yesterday, the kittens *lay* on the blankets in the laundry room.

The past participle of a verb tells that the action began in the past and was completed in the past. In order to form the past participle, the verb must be preceded by one of the following verbs: *was, were, has, had,* or *have.*
Mother *has laid* her briefcase on the same table every night for years.
The cats *have lain* in the same windowsill every evening.

Identify It
Write whether the forms of *lay* and *lie* mean *to place* or *to recline.* Write a **P** for *place* and an **R** for *recline.*

1. __R__ Don t lie in the sun without sunscreen!
2. __P__ It was unusual the papers were missing; he had laid them in the same spot every morning.
3. __R__ Meagan and Ashley had lain in the sun too long.
4. __P__ Jean laid the covers over the plates before the rain hit.
5. __P__ Please lay the cups and plates at the end of the table.
6. __R__ The toddlers lay down for a long nap earlier today.
7. __P__ Don t lay your homework by your computer, you ll forget about it in the morning.
8. __R__ Lie on the blanket on the sand.
9. __P__ Barbara laid her blanket near the bed.
10. __R__ Maggie lay down for a quick nap yesterday.

120

Page 121

Complete It
Complete the following sentences by circling the best answers in parentheses.

1. Patrick has (laid, (lain)) on his arm too long and has lost feeling in it.
2. The exercisers ((lay,) lie) their towels in the basket on their way out.
3. I like to (lay, (lie)) down for a few minutes before dinner.
4. The writer ((laid,) lay) down his pen when he finished.
5. The same architects have ((laid,) lain) out the plans every year.
6. Mr. Shaloub has ((laid,) lain) out the homework assignments on the work table.
7. The sleeping turtle has (laid, (lain)) in the same spot for hours.
8. "Please ((lay,) lie) your homework assignments on my desk," said the teacher.
9. We poured club soda on the stain in the carpet and let it ((lay,) lie) for several minutes.
10. The picnickers ((laid,) lay) the lunch boxes on the tablecloth before the wind blew it away.

Try It
Write six sentences of your own. Write one sentence for each of the forms of *lie* and *lay*.

1. _____
2. _____
3. _____
4. _____ Answers will vary. _____
5. _____
6. _____

121

Page 122

Remember that adjectives modify nouns. **Comparative adjectives** compare two nouns and **superlative adjectives** compare three or more nouns.
    busy/busier/busiest   early/earlier/earliest   easy/easier/easiest

Notice that these adjectives change **y** to **i** before adding the suffixes **—er** for comparatives or **—est** for superlatives.

Describing one noun:
    The corner of 4th Street and Main Street is a *busy* intersection.
    Let's go to the *early* movie.
    This is an *easy* assignment.

Comparing two nouns:
    The store on this side of town is *busier* than the store across town.
    I'll go to an *earlier* show and let you know how it is.
    The pasta salad looks like an *easier* recipe than the potato salad.

Comparing three or more nouns:
    The end of school is the *busiest* time of year.
    Whoever leaves *earliest* will get the best seats.
    I want to take the *easiest* way home.

Match It
Draw a line to match the sentence blanks in Column A with the adjectives in Column B.

Column A	Column B
1. Of the three assignments, this one is the ___easiest___.	busy
2. Reading all of these chapters will keep me very ___busy___.	busier
3. I'll take the ___earlier___ of the two classes so I'll finish sooner.	busiest
4. Because of the deadlines, I'm ___busier___ this week than next.	early
5. It's an ___early___ game, so we'll be home for dinner.	earlier
6. I'm tired; I want to take the ___easier___ of the two exercise classes.	earliest
7. The ___busiest___ days are when I both work and go to school.	easy
8. The ___earliest___ of all the busses will get us there on time.	easier
9. I only have one assignment; it's an ___easy___ day.	easiest

122

Page 123

Proof It
Proofread the following biography. Correct the errors made in the use of adjectives. Not all of the adjectives are from this lesson.

> ᴇ — deletes incorrect letters, words, punctuation
> ʌ — inserts correct letters, words, punctuation

Lance Armstrong

Riding more than 2,000 miles in all kinds of weather and through some of the
highest
world's ~~high~~ mountains, Lance Armstrong has earned a spot as one of the world's
greatest
~~greater~~ sports figures. The road to the yellow jersey (the shirt worn by the winner of the
                    easy
Tour de France) wasn't an ~~easier~~ one.
                         early
At a young age, he tried football and swimming. He even rose ~~earlier~~ every

morning to ride his bicycle 20 miles to swimming practice. He entered and won his first
                            early
triathlon at age 13. It was clear ~~earlier~~ on that he excelled at bicycling. He became
busier   busy
~~busy~~ than most of his friends as he competed in many races. Armstrong got ~~busier~~ and

became a world-class cyclist.

Tragedy hit when Armstrong was 25. Doctors found he had cancer. After many

operations, Armstrong survived. He was more determined than ever to prove his
                                     easy
sportsmanship. Armstrong never took the ~~easier~~ way out; he started training even

harder! He won his first Tour de France in 1999 the only cancer survivor to win a Tour de

France. Lance Armstrong is more than just a sports figure: he is a sports hero and legend.

Try It
Write a paragraph about one of your heroes. Use at least one of the forms of each *busy*, *easy*, and *early*.

_____ Answers will vary. _____

123

Page 124

Comparative and **superlative adjectives** can also be formed by adding the words *more* (comparative) and *most* (superlative) before the adjective. The words *more* and *most* are used instead of adding the endings **—er** and **—est** to longer adjectives.
    The sunrise today was even *more beautiful* than the one yesterday.
    It was the *most magnificent* sunrise of any I'd ever seen.

The adjectives *good* and *bad* have their own rules.
    That was a *good* movie that we saw last night.
    It looks like there will even be a *better* one out next weekend.
    But neither will be the *best* movie of all time.

    Remove the *bad* apples from the basket.
    The *worse* of the two pies were made with bad apples.
    It was the *worst* pie I had ever eaten.

Identify It
Identify the following sentences by writing a **C** for comparative or an **S** for superlative.

1. __S__ The alexandrite, June's birthstone, is one of the most rare gemstones.
2. __C__ The red garnet, the birthstone of January, is more popular than the green garnet.
3. __S__ The best peridots, the August birthstone, have a greenish-yellowish color.
4. __S__ The most expensive color of sapphires, September's stone, is blue.
5. __C__ Because of its color variety, tourmalines, the birthstone of October, have become more popular in recent years.
6. __C__ A real aquamarine has much better quality than its synthetic substitute.
7. __S__ Some of the most beautiful shades of purple are found in the February birthstone, amethyst.
8. __C__ Fine emeralds, the birthstone of May, are more rare than fine diamonds.
9. __S__ The most popular gemstone is the diamond, April's birthstone.
10. __S__ The July birthstone, ruby, is known to celebrate the most special occasions.
11. __S__ Most topaz, the November birthstone, come in many soft colors.
12. __S__ The December birthstone, zircon, is one of the most recent additions to the list of common gems.

124

Answer Key

Page 133

Match It
Draw a line to match the words in Column A with their contractions in Column B. These contractions are not on the list, but follow the same patterns.

Column A	Column B
1. she is or she has	might've
2. would have	they'll
3. might have	they'd
4. he will	weren't
5. they will	she's
6. he would or he had	hadn't
7. they would or they had	couldn't
8. could not	he'd
9. were not	would've
10. had not	he'll

Try It
Write a sentence for each of the contractions in the activity above. Be sure to use the contraction form of the words.

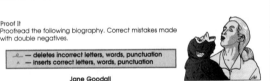

Answers will vary.

133

Page 134

A **negative** sentence states the opposite. Negative words include *not, no, never, nobody, nowhere, nothing, barely, hardly,* and *scarcely;* and contractions containing the word *not.*

Double negatives happen when two negative words are used in the same sentence. Don't use double negatives; it will make your sentence positive again, and it is poor grammar.

Negative: We *won't* go anywhere without you.
Double Negative: We *won't* go *nowhere* without you.

Negative: I *never* like to ride my bike after dark.
Double Negative: I *don't never* like to ride my bike after dark.

Negative: I can *hardly* wait until baseball season.
Double Negative: I *can't hardly* wait until baseball season.

Rewrite It
Rewrite the following sentences. Correct the sentence if it contains a double negative.

1. I love breakfast; I can't imagine not skipping it.
   I love breakfast; I can't imagine skipping it.
2. I can't scarcely believe I made it all the way down the slope without falling.
   I scarcely believe I made it all the way down the slope without falling.
3. Samantha doesn't never like to wear her coat outside.
   Samantha doesn't like to wear her coat outside.
4. The class hasn't received their report cards yet.
   The class hasn't received their report cards yet.
5. I'm not going nowhere until it stops raining.
   I'm going nowhere until it stops raining.
6. Paul has barely nothing to contribute to the argument.
   Paul has nothing to contribute to the argument.
7. Sarah never reveals her secrets.
   Sarah never reveals her secrets.
8. I don't think nobody can make it to the event early.
   I think nobody can make it to the event early.

134

Page 135

Proof It
Proofread the following biography. Correct mistakes made with double negatives.

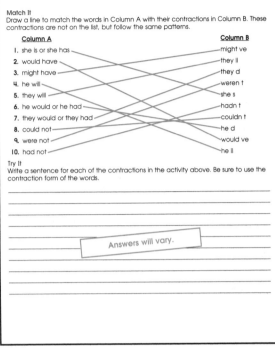

| — deletes incorrect letters, words, punctuation |
| ^ — inserts correct letters, words, punctuation |

Jane Goodall

As a young girl, Jane Goodall knew she wanted to work with chimpanzees. She fulfilled her dream; although at the time (early 1960s) it was not ~~scarcely~~ common for women to work in Africa. At the time, nobody ~~couldn't~~ or have dreamed of the success she would have with the chimpanzees of Tanzania. When the chimps first noticed Goodall in the forests, they didn't ~~never~~ stay close. Goodall didn't ~~never~~ give up.

many (or any)
Before this time, it was not believed by ~~nobody~~ that chimpanzees and other animals have personalities, but Goodall recorded proof. Goodall even witnessed one family of chimps adopt an orphan baby.

The Jane Goodall Institute for Wildlife Research, Education, and Conservation supports continuing study on wild chimpanzees. However, it is ~~not hardly~~ just about
not (or hardly)
research. The institute promotes community-centered development programs and habitat protection efforts in Africa.

Try It
Write six negative sentences using each of the following words: *not, never, nobody, nowhere, nothing, barely, hardly,* and *scarcely.*

Answers will vary.

135

Page 136

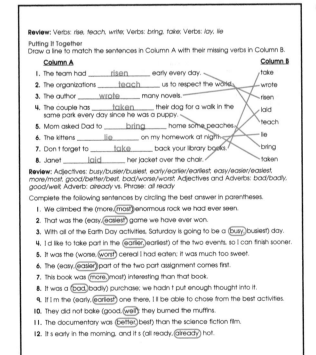

Review: Verbs: *rise, teach, write;* Verbs: *bring, take;* Verbs: *lay, lie*

Putting It Together
Draw a line to match the sentences in Column A with their missing verbs in Column B.

Column A	Column B
1. The team had ___ risen ___ early every day.	take
2. The organizations ___ teach ___ us to respect the world.	wrote
3. The author ___ wrote ___ many novels.	risen
4. The couple has ___ taken ___ their dog for a walk in the same park every day since he was a puppy.	laid
5. Mom asked Dad to ___ bring ___ home some peaches.	teach
6. The kittens ___ lie ___ on my homework at night.	lie
7. Don't forget to ___ take ___ back your library books.	bring
8. Janet ___ laid ___ her jacket over the chair.	taken

Review: Adjectives: *busy/busier/busiest, early/earlier/earliest, easy/easier/easiest, more/most, good/better/best, bad/worse/worst;* Adjectives and Adverbs: *bad/badly, good/well;* Adverb: *already* vs. Phrase: *all ready*

Complete the following sentences by circling the best answer in parentheses.

1. We climbed the (more, (most)) enormous rock we had ever seen.
2. That was the (easy, (easiest)) game we have ever won.
3. With all of the Earth Day activities, Saturday is going to be a ((busy), busiest) day.
4. I'd like to take part in the ((earlier), earliest) of the two events, so I can finish sooner.
5. It was the (worse, (worst)) cereal I had eaten; it was much too sweet.
6. The ((easy), easier) part of the two part assignment comes first.
7. This book was ((more), most) interesting than that book.
8. It was a ((bad), badly) purchase; we hadn't put enough thought into it.
9. If I'm the (early, (earliest)) one there, I'll be able to chose from the best activities.
10. They did not bake (good, (well)); they burned the muffins.
11. The documentary was ((better), best) than the science fiction film.
12. It's early in the morning, and it's (all ready, (already)) hot.

136

Review: Homophones: *cereal/serial, coarse/course, council/counsel, overseas/oversees, ring/wring, cent/scent/sent*; Contractions; Negatives/Double Negatives

If the sentence correctly uses homophones, contractions, and double negatives, write a **C** on the line. If the sentence incorrectly uses homophones, contractions, or uses double negatives, write an **X** on the line. Then, write the word that would correctly complete the sentence.

1. Sydney likes raisins and granola in his cereal. __C__ _____
2. That material was too course for Judy. __X__ ____coarse____
3. The counsel meets twice a week. __X__ ____council____
4. Mitzi s going overseas to visit her friends. __C__ _____
5. Lynn bought herself a beautiful ring. __C__ _____
6. Rebecca wouldn t even pay a sent for that material. __X__ ____cent____
7. The magazine articles Nathan s writing will be released as a cereal. __X__ ____serial____
8. Debbie ran on a beautiful tree-lined coarse around a lake. __X__ ____course____
9. Greg will council his staff on the new project. __X__ ____counsel____
10. Dr. Henry, the senior veterinarian, overseas the veterinary students. __X__ ____oversees____
11. Please ring out the towels before placing them in the dryer. __X__ ____wring____
12. Stacy liked the sent of the flowers in the window box. __X__ ____scent____
13. Elizabeth cent in her application to the coffee shop. __X__ ____sent____
14. Le ts stop for pizza after our ride. __X__ ____Let s____
15. Our teacher told us to never stop learning. __C__ _____

137

Notes

Notes